T0067434

CLAIM YOUR
RIGHTFUL
PLACE

Own the Space You Occupy by Practicing
Your New Future Every Day

Madeleen Viljoen-Theron

BALBOA.
PRESS

A DIVISION OF HAY HOUSE

Scripture quoted by permission. Quotations designated (NET) are from The NET Bible® Copyright © 2005 by Biblical Studies Press, L.L.C. www.bible.org All rights reserved.

Balboa Press books may be ordered through booksellers or by contacting:

Balboa Press
A Division of Hay House
1663 Liberty Drive
Bloomington, IN 47403
www.balboapress.com
1 (877) 407-4847

Because of the dynamic nature of the Internet, any web addresses or links contained in this book may have changed since publication and may no longer be valid. The views expressed in this work are solely those of the author and do not necessarily reflect the views of the publisher, and the publisher hereby disclaims any responsibility for them.

The author of this book does not dispense medical advice or prescribe the use of any technique as a form of treatment for physical, emotional, or medical problems without the advice of a physician, either directly or indirectly. The intent of the author is only to offer information of a general nature to help you in your quest for emotional and spiritual well-being. In the event you use any of the information in this book for yourself, which is your constitutional right, the author and the publisher assume no responsibility for your actions.

Any people depicted in stock imagery provided by Thinkstock are models, and such images are being used for illustrative purposes only. Certain stock imagery © Thinkstock.

Print information available on the last page.

ISBN: 978-1-5043-7446-0 (sc)
ISBN: 978-1-5043-7447-7 (e)

Balboa Press rev. date: 02/13/2017

TABLE OF CONTENTS

FOREWORD

When I contemplate life on earth, I realize that we are wandering through time and space without awareness of the significance of life, and we do not acknowledge the ingenuousness and wonder of the creation we are bound to. I have to ask the question; what if life is actually about change, about growing that part of your spirit that is in need of an upgrade. It takes courage to investigate yourself, acknowledging your shortcomings and making an effort to change and better yourself. I think we are supposed to undergo some sort of metamorphosis throughout our lives, maybe even more than once.

Claiming my rightful place in this life and owning the space I occupy was literally the most difficult thing I had to learn to do. I suffered for a very long time from a false sense of unworthiness and it had a negative effect on my physical, emotional and spiritual wellbeing. I think our self-professed failures and inability to achieve lasting success can be directly linked to our failure in claiming our rightful place, owning the space we occupy, and standing up for ourselves. We fail to truly believe that we are good enough to deserve the very best and we neglect to practice our new proposed future every day. We have been manipulated for centuries into believing that we are powerless and should put our trust in other people and the world around us. We were never taught to trust in our inner guidance until recently, and now is the time to step it up a notch.

When you become self-aware - aware of whom you really are, the space you occupy, and the magnificence of your true capabilities, you will be able to shed the old skin of wrong belief systems and fear. You will start to claim your rightful place, occupy the space you're in, even better - own the space you occupy. You'll be comfortable in your own skin. Ignorance of what is going on in this world will keep you in mental, emotional and physical slavery. It is time to wake up.

You must become aware of the fact that it always has been, and still are, people like us that are making the rules of how we should be living our lives, and I am not referring to God's laws or the laws of a land. We have to realize that we are the people and we can therefore change rules, make new ones, or at least create our own set of rules of how we should be living our lives. I am not referring to unlawfulness, because that is not the way to true freedom.

I used to think of all the excuses in the world why I should not start this book, nevertheless completing it, but alas! I had no choice but to start and finish it, although it took me a couple of years. My inner spirit kept on nagging me, so here it is – Claim your rightful place and own the space you occupy by practicing your new future every day, to assist you in your transition of becoming a free-thinking person. The road you are about to embark on is not easy. It is filled with road bumps, but you have to persist. You have to practice your new future EVERY day; that's the key.

The words; 'own the space you occupy' might seem strange to you since you are on this earth, so don't you naturally own the space you occupy? Well, yes and no. Yes, you are here on earth occupying space, and the space you occupy moves with you wherever you go, but are you really taking ownership of the fact that you are here for a reason? Are you happy to be here? Do you feel you belong here and that you have the right to be alive and have a wonderful, prosperous life? Are you really claiming your rightful place, or do you shy away and say; excuse me, pardon me, oh poor me, the whole world is against me? Are you merely drifting through life like tumbleweed that's been tossed around in the wind? Neither here, nor there, unclear of who you are or who you're supposed to be? Then it's a clear; NO, you are not claiming your rightful place and you definitely do not own the space you occupy.

Don't feel alone. There are many people that are going through the same motions. I was like that - constantly moving out of the way to make space for people I thought were better than me, more blessed and more worthy to inhabit the earth. I made space for the more fortunate, more beautiful, more rich and powerful. For some reason I felt polluted; even when I was physically clean it was never enough. I had a constant feeling that I have to transform into something, but I did not know what and it was driving me crazy! I realized that I was suffering from a serious lack of self-confidence, and that any self-confidence I was able to muster was short-lived. The media did not help. We are constantly bombarded with other people's ideas of how amazingly rich, beautiful, slim and successful we should be. People and circumstances are being blown out of proportion and we never get the chance to really find ourselves. It is impossible to live up to another peoples' standards.

I was constantly waiting for something great to happen to me; or for someone great and powerful to tell me what I should or should not do, and that I am okay. What nonsense! I am the something great, I am the worthy one, and so are you; otherwise you would not be here. Therefore I say to you; Claim your Rightful place and own the space you occupy, because you are worthy to do just that! How do you claim your rightful place and owning it? By practicing your new future every day!

There seem to be a lot of physical evidence that this task could be close to impossible, and that is exactly why this book took so long to see the light – there's so much to say, and even then it would still be incomplete. In this book I started from where I think things go wrong for most people, and that is from birth. What you were taught since the day you were born are the key influences that determine how you are thinking about yourself and about life in general today. It determines what you are practicing in your daily life and how you process the signals from outside. It literally took years and years of struggling through this myself to be able to pin it down. Most of my life I had the feeling that I must somehow reach a higher form of existence or I fear I would've gone mad. I had to force myself to come to the true realization of who I am and I had to start believing that I am good enough, that I am worthy, and that I can do and be anything I want – that I could claim my rightful place on this earth! Deep down inside of me I always knew that I would never be truly happy unless I've done just that.

The late Dr. Wayne W Dyer said the following in his book, 'Wishes fulfilled,' 'Allow yourself to follow your dreams and encourage your imagination by having a mind that is open to everything and attached to nothing.' It was a long road, and it is not yet finished, but I will race it till the end. I want to be able to say that 'I have fought a good fight, I have finished my course, and I have kept the faith.' 2 Timothy 4:7.

***

All Bible references were taken from the New English Translation (NET), unless otherwise indicated.

THANK YOU AND DEDICATION

I want to thank my son; Vincente Armand Viljoen. You are the greatest man I know. Thank you for believing in me and for your encouragement. You share my passion for a changed world. You are my main reason for being here, and my inspiration.

To Adriaan Louis Theron, thank you for giving me the time and space to follow my dreams.

Throughout this book you'll find quotes and articles that were taken from the Wakeup-world.com website, and from Hay House published books. I want to thank the authors from whom I was able to borrow infinite wisdom and valuable information, especially Dr. Wayne W Dyer (1940 - 2015). Your book, 'The Power of Intention,' was the first motivational self-help book I read, and that was where my journey started.

I thank God the Father, Jesus Christ and the Holy Spirit, who are always there to encourage and guide me. This book is dedicated to you.

THE PHYSICAL WORLD

The physical world is the beginning of our awareness, it is not our enemy. It was created to accommodate and serve us, all of it. That's why plants and animals were created before man, so it could be ready, waiting for us to rule over. You need the physical world to survive. Crucial resources might have been hijacked by unknown greedy forces, and whether they are in or out of this world does not really make a difference.

For the purpose of this book I am going to refer to these greedy forces as 'the enemy.' You are let to believe that life is mainly a struggle for survival, but it is a lie. There was a time that it might've been true, but that was before Christ's deliverance and He urges us in James 4:7 to 'submit ourselves to God and resist the devil, because the devil (enemy) will then flee from us.' The question is; why then are we still living as if nothing happened to change our fate? Something did happen, but most people are still blindly chained to a life of physical, mental and emotional slavery. Here is a hint; 'Do not be conformed to this present world, but be transformed by the renewing of your mind, so that you may test and approve what is the will of God - what is good and well-pleasing and perfect.' Romans 2:12.

As long as you have not claimed your *own* rightful place, and as long as you are still sharing the same mind as the rest of the world, you will remain as is, chained. You have to stand up for yourself and say 'enough is enough, I am claiming my rightful place, and I am renewing my mind so I can experience true liberation!' The enemy has found a way to cloud our minds and blind us from the truth by keeping us busy with the daily, mundane tide of life – eating, sleeping, working, worrying about finances or something else, stressing, or whatever else we do on a daily basis. We're on autopilot like a programmed robot. We have to wake up and realize that we can stop this endless cycle. You can change your life. As a matter of fact, it is God's will that you become the free person whom you were created to be, and that you are free from oppression and slavery. There is no need to continue believing that only sparsity and hardship exist. The physical world is not your enemy.

I am not going to lie and say that there will be no challenges in your life, but bear with me. You will come to understand what I mean later in this book. The thing is; you have what you need on all levels of existence, and when you believe this rather than the opposite, everything you require for survival will be there when you need it, and that is where believing in yourself and in God comes in. It is difficult to receive when you are in a state of worry or fear, and that is what the enemy is feeding on, your worries and your fear. It keeps you from the fullness of life, from abundance and from God. The law of attraction is always at work; what you sow you reap and what you believe in, you attract.

Without the physical world, material things, animals, plants, trees and people, we will cease to exist. These are the things that give meaning to our lives. It is your choice if you want to chase only after the material things in life by accumulating wealth rather than having a holistic experience on every level of existence. If you focus too hard on one aspect life has to offer you might lose track of all the other wonderful experiences you can have. There has to be a balance. You were created to experience life to the fullest and enjoy everything you do while you are living out your purpose. You are an expression of the Creator and He finds pleasure in your existence, on all levels. What will the purpose of being alive be if you are unable to enjoy life? Do you really think you are here to suffer? That's a lie straight from the pits of hell. A lie that you were told since the day you were born, but worse than that, the lie goes back hundreds, maybe thousands, of years.

Why do you think Christ was sent? To save us from ourselves, to forgive our sins; re-instate our status with the Father through His sacrifice, to teach us how to live life without worries and fear, to trust ourselves and Him in everything we do? Yes to all of it, and to deliver us from the oppressors of this world, to snatch us form the claws of the condemned, whether physical or spiritual, human of alien – the enemy. Unfortunately we are in the middle of a battle between good and evil, but don't be scared. Although the enemy wants your life, God will not allow it, unless you do - it is your choice. Before the 'great fall of humanity' we were one with creation, the universe and God, but we lost the unity. Restoration took place through Christ, but most people still have to grasp the concept and decide to renew their minds. It is the 'how do I renew my mind' that the enemy has found a way to keep from humanity. The time for change has however arrived!

If you believe that you have all you need and that everything is provided for, that everything on this earth were created for you so you can fashion a life for yourself here because you are human, and if you are happy and content, the enemy has no hold on you - that is why you've been lied to, so you can stay in physical, spiritual and emotional bondage, slavery and fear, which will cloud your mind – your most powerful tool, and so that you are unable to claim your rightful place on this earth! If you cede your rightful place by doubting your existence, the enemy has a hold on you and evil has won.

Why does the enemy want you to cede your rightful place? So you can continue working harder to keep the fake monetary system going and forget what is important; to forget who you are and why you are here, and so that you will become a lost soul. Remember, the battle is between good and evil and we are in the middle of it, pawns on the chess board of life. It is important for you to claim your rightful place and tell the enemy off – own the space you occupy! You must further understand that Christ's role of deliverance is tightly interwoven in all of this. If you choose to believe in Him, and to trust Him with your life, the enemy has to back off.

If there are life lessons you need to learn to help you on your journey of becoming who you're supposed to be, you will acquire them by experience, good or bad, not by artificial inseminated oppression and suffering. I say again; the physical world we live in is not our enemy, and the law of attraction is not opposed to believing in God, Jesus Christ, a higher being, or in a universal force, it's all interwoven, part of one big whole.

A CLEAR LINK

Believing in the law of attraction is not opposed to believing in God, Jesus Christ, a higher being, or a universal force. It is interwoven, part of one whole.

With the state the world is in today, there seem to be more and more people that doubt that God, or any other form of 'higher being' exists. They do not believe that Christ was sent to the earth to save us from ourselves and from the wicked. I don't blame them for doubting. Each person who has a different opinion starts his or her own movement or chooses to have no part in any of this. Every culture has a different religion, and it seems that in every culture prayers are answered, go figure! How is that possible if they do not believe in the same God as you? Can you hear yourself? What does it matter wat other people are doing? Focus on your own life because you are the one that will have to give an account for the way you lived your life.

The enemy thrives on all forms of division since division takes your attention away from what is really important and from yourself, the most important person on this earth. It is not selfish to regard yourself as such, because if you are not taking care of yourself first you won't be able to take care of anybody else. You cannot give what you do not have. If you feel physically, mentally or emotionally unwell it will be hard for you to care of another person, it is therefore crucial that you take care of yourself on all these levels before you can take care of others. Taking care of your own wellbeing is not the same as being selfish. It is, however, possible to care for others while you are in the process of building yourself up.

Today there are as many beliefs as there are people. So, whom should you follow? Whose ideas and teachings are the truth? Whom can you trust? The multitude of different beliefs and religious institutions are confusing to those who believe in God, and even more so to the non-believers! Can you see that this might be a plan in the making; create confusion and panic? This is the plan of the evil one, the enemy. Divide people, let them differ in fundamental ways and hate each other. Let them fight over what is wrong and what is right. Confuse the masses; artificially inseminate anger, hate and fear. Make them doubt that a higher power exists. Help them to be consumed with every-day life, with the trivial pursuit of what they will eat, drink and what clothes they will wear. Mission accomplished! It is time to wake up world.

I want to offer a spark of hope in all of this chaos, and that is that there's a clear link between all the belief systems and religions in this world, and that is faith. Faith is the single most powerful thing you can possess. In Mark 11:23 we read the following, 'I tell you the truth, if someone say to this mountain, 'Be lifted up and thrown into the sea,' and do not doubt in his heart, but believe that what he says will happen, it will be done for him,' and in Matthew 17:20, 'He told them, 'It was because of your little faith. I tell you the truth, if you have faith the size of a mustard seed, you will say to this mountain, 'Move from here to there,' and it will move; nothing will be impossible for you.' These are two very powerful statements. Imagine if you were taught the value of faith and how to practice faith from a very young age - there would've been a lot of mountains in the sea! I promise you, our lives and our whole world would've been different. With real faith it would've bee possible to grow enough food for everyone, and everybody would've been able to live a happy and prosperous life.

Faith is complete trust or confidence in someone or something. Choose wisely in what or whom you put your faith. Faith is none other than the law of attraction. What you believe to be true will be true for you in your life – what you believe or have faith in, you will attract to yourself because you believe it - faith as small as a mustard seed can cause you to move a mountain! Believing in the law of attraction is not opposed to believing in God, Christ, a higher being, or in a universal force, it's all interwoven, part of one whole – a clear link. Belief is a very strong force, and it is linked to faith. The law of attraction means what you have faith in, or what you believe, you will get. The question you should ask yourself is; 'Who is in charge of my life, the enemy, God, or I?'

WHO IS IN CHARGE OF YOUR LIFE?

ontrary to popular belief, God is not in charge of your life and neither is the enemy. You are. You are the only person that is able to make a choice for yourself; therefore you are in charge of you. There is a difference in believing in God's ability to help you and guide you with the help of His Holy Spirit and believing that something or someone outside of yourself is in charge of your life. You already have the authority to conquer according to Luke 10:19 that says, 'Look, I have given you authority to tread on snakes and scorpions and on the full force of the enemy, and nothing will hurt you.' What a liberating thought.

It is impossible for God, who is spirit, to make up or change your mind, to stop you from eating the foods that make you fat, to stop you from biting your nails, or for Him to say no to drugs on your behalf. He cannot force you to have self-confidence, to be an honest person, to learn for your exams, or to be kind. Only you can do all of that. It is time to take responsibility for your actions and your choices. You are in charge of you. Guidance was placed inside of you, it is called instinct or your gut feeling, and it warns you when something is wrong. You always know what is going on, even if you choose to ignore it. The way things turn out is ultimately up to you and not up to God, whether you believe it or not.

The time for God's spirit has arrived! Wake up world, and listen! His spirit is inside you and will guide you in all things. It is therefore important to believe in yourself, claim your rightful place, own the space you occupy, think appropriate thoughts, speak the right words, believe in the law of attraction and in sowing and reaping, and to trust God and have faith. You have to understand that you and God are one. You are a three dimensional being just as He is. You are body, mind (soul), and spirit, whereas he is God, Jesus Christ and the Holy Spirit. You are a 'chip off the old block.'

The following information will empower you to take charge of your own life if you thus far allowed the outside world to run it for you; everything in life is energy, sound and vibration, even when it appears to be solid. For your vibrating, energy spirit to survive here on earth it required a physical body. You are not to consider yourself as a solid physical being, but rather a spirit-being in a physical energy-body. Consider this; as a vibrational being you attract into your life those things which you are vibrationally equal to. If you do not like what you have on any level of existence, physically, spiritually or emotionally, you need to lovingly, without force, change your frequency. We will discuss how you can change your frequency later in this book. You can't blame God for anything that goes wrong in your life, rather praise Him for everything that goes well, everything, even when you say no to drugs or alcohol, or stop biting your nails. What you practice every day becomes part of your life, and gratefulness is one of the key components for success. Funny, isn't it? It is easier to blame someone else for the wrong than for the good. When it's good, it is all you, but when it's bad, it's someone else, or God. Let me tell you, it is ALL YOU. You are doing the good and the bad to yourself. It is time to take responsibility.

There was a time I used to speculate about the existence of God. I was wondering if He really existed because I made the mistake of listening to the opinions of others. There are so many questions and speculations; is God male or female, did He create everything or was it evolution, or a big bang? What I nearly missed was the fact that He created everything through the spoken word, which is sound and vibration, and that the spoken word he used was Jesus Christ whom he was forced to send later in the flesh so we can get the message, since we tend to experience things only with our physical senses, until we choose to wake up.

'Christ' means that God himself ordained a person and has given him authority to act as His representative, which means if you believe in the Christ who was sent as the Creator's representative, whom is also His Word (vibration), you will be recognized as belonging to God, and therefore saved from the enemy. The enemy and his allies are currently ruling the physical world, but for you to believe in God, you must also first believe in yourself. If you do not believe in yourself, your vibrational frequency will be weak, and that will be a sign to the enemy that you are available to prey on. When your vibration is strong, and in sync with His Word (vibration), which is Christ – His representative, the enemy has to leave you alone. You are 'unavailable' to prey on.

God used sound and vibration - words, to create everything. His Word (Jesus Christ) is an integral part of Him, and He had to separate it for a short while so we can experience it in the flesh. When all was lost due to the enemy's interference, He had to re-establish the connection between Himself and us by sending His Word to the earth to conquer death and thereby the enemy who wants the human race dead, extinct, so he can take over the earth together with his demons. And believe me; the enemy also has human collaborators on this earth.

I believe that God the Father exists, the Creator of all things – the earth, everything above and below it - the whole universe. I believe that He wants you to believe in yourself, and to claim your rightful place and own the space you occupy. You have to do this. I believe that He guides us through His Spirit, and that is why we instinctively know what is right and what is wrong. What you do with the knowledge is called choice and that is yours and yours alone. God has nothing to do with the choices you make; His Spirit can only guide you.

There is a place for praying and believing and trusting, and it links up with 'what you think and believe in your heart, so it will be for you.' It is not a new concept. It is not 'New Age thinking.' This truth is older than the Bible itself. The sad part is that some children are raised in front of the television and in shopping malls, instead of their parents spending wholesome time with their children so they can pass on these ancient truths. God is not the enemy and darkness has never prevailed against the light. Why would you deliberately choose the wrong side? You have to get God on your side, as a matter of fact, He is already on your side – 'If you remain in me and my words remain in you, ask whatever you want, and it will be done for you.' John 15:7. Now how is that for powerful words?

Thinking that God is in charge of your life equals not taking responsibility for your own life and thereby seeking an escape goat to blame when something goes wrong. I do not say He is not there to guide you, but it is still you that will be making the final choices. You will have to live with the consequences of your choices – sow and reap, expect and get - the law of attraction. The time has come to wake up and realize your role in shaping your life.

WHERE DOES GOD FIT IN?

In my search for freedom I found myself closer to God than ever before!

We love to declare our independence, but whether we like it or not, there is always a Higher Power at work. It exists with or without our acknowledgement. Even an atheist believes in something, even if it is only in himself. Relying only on yourself - your own strength and insights might work for a while, but eventually you will start doubting yourself, or things will go wrong and you'll feel lost and alone because there is no back-up. When things fall apart is not the time to start asking for divine guidance. You have to ask for it every day! Trusting only in yourself can become a big burden. It is comforting to have someone other than yourself to trust and rely on, someone that has your back, and since humans are immensely fallible, it is best to have God on your side, and you do – believe it!

As a human being you are worthy of God's attention, and it is important that you realize and believe that. He loves us the same way we love our own children. You can communicate with Him at any time, the whole time if you want to - some call it prayer, but do not think of prayer the way you were taught as a child. Prayer is way more than that; it is forming a relationship with God. You can speak to Him about everything, all day long – He loves that! Human relationships are formed through communication; the same is said for your relationship with the divine. Don't overthink it and make it complicated, because it is not.

Making use of the modern term 'mind power,' which is positive thinking by choosing your thoughts and speaking and acting in alignment with that, in other words; practicing your new future, is not in opposition with what God wants from you at all - 'Whatever is true, whatever is worthy of respect, whatever is just, whatever is pure, whatever is lovely, whatever is commendable, if something is excellent or praiseworthy, think about these things.' Philippians 4:8. Using mind power is a necessary step in realizing what God wants from you, because you can block His voice and guidance through negativity. God hates to be ignored. In whatever you do, you have to acknowledge and honor Him.

The Divine guides you through His Spirit, and anyone has access to it, even you. When you ask for guidance through prayer, or any other way, become still so you can know the answer within yourself because that is where His spirit dwells. That is the reason you have to believe in yourself! You and God are one; therefore believing in yourself is the same as believing in Him, and that is the door to your successful new future of freedom and abundance! We tend to believe what we were taught as a child, and unfortunately we've been taught that God is a separate entity from us. He is not, and neither is everything else. We are all part of one whole. It is only difficult to accept this because we are not use to the concept. Even though God is part of us, He still allows us to make our own choices. If you, however, listen to His guidance, you will make the right choices. Life is not a clear-cut black and white canvas; it is more complicated than that. It is more like a multi-layered, magnificent, colorful painting with a lot of different dimensions.

I don't think we realize how much God loves us. Only when we allow all things - good and bad, to teach us about ourselves, we will be able to comprehend His Divine guidance behind it all. Even when we disregard His initial guidance and follow our own heads by making the wrong choices, He makes sure it works out to our benefit in the end. I have seen this in my own life numerous times!

In his book, '21 Days to master success & inner peace,' Dr. Wayne W Dyer said the following, 'There is no place that God is not. Remind yourself of this every day. It has been said that God sleeps in the minerals, rests in the vegetables, walks in the animals, and thinks in us. Think of God as a presence rather than a person, a presence that allows a seed to sprout, that moves the stars across the sky, and simultaneously moves a thought across your mind. A presence that grows the grass and grows your fingernails all at the same time. This presence is everywhere; therefore, it must also be in you! And if it's everywhere, it must be in all that you perceive to be missing from your life. In some inexplicable way, you're already connected to all that you'd like to attract into your life by the presence of this universal, all-powerful Spirit called God.'

We can try to resist the fact that there is a God, but sooner or later we will get our senses back and realize that it is not such a bad thing.

INNER STRUGGLE

For as long as I can remember I've struggled with low self-esteem, an inferiority complex, and being fearful of everything. It was clear to me that I have not yet claimed *my* rightful place on this earth. My vibrational frequency kept on going in and out, on and off. I was literally non-existing to the universe - I was a weak signal!

The fact that I had a difficult, unsupported childhood did not help much. As I grew up I got immensely tired of struggling and fighting against what 'I did not want.' These unwanted things kept on piling up because I did not yet have knowledge about the concept that I (my mind) was the one responsible for my hardships, or about the law of attraction and belief. I was under the impression that all bad things happen to people without them having any say about it, so I kept on crying and yearning for liberation and inner peace. When I first heard about the notion that I was the one responsible for my struggles, I did not dismiss the idea outright; although I did not like the idea that I was responsible, I decided to embraced it because it meant I had some amount of control over my life which I, up until then, thought I did not have. The feeling of having no control over what happens to you is far worse than realizing that you yourself are responsible.

I had to learn to let go, especially of the past. Each passing second belongs to the past. Letting go does not mean you are giving up on life, but here's the thing; the more you struggle, the tighter the negative side of live squeezes you, like a flesh-eating plant. The insect's struggle is what activates the plant to squeeze tighter, and that is how life is, so stop struggling! The biggest hardship for me was to live in the reality of the physical world. As a matter of fact, at one time I hated being alive. It is a strong statement, but I have to be true to myself, and to you. I think there are a lot of people that feel the same way but they do not know what to do about it. Even the way nature, animals and children are treated in this world caused me daily physical and emotional pain and heartache. I've reached a point where I couldn't stand it anymore and I felt that I must somehow reach a higher form of existence, otherwise I feared I might've gone mad!

I've been searching for inner peace and my place in this life for a very long time, always striving to become a better version of myself, trying to justify my existence, but at the same time feeling as if I was failing miserably! The more I attempted to reach that unattainable goal, the more I had to continue striving. I felt like I've managed to make a good mess of everything – unhappy childhood, unfulfilling jobs, failed marriages, constantly depressed and miserable, with only small glimpses here and there of how life should be. The thought of ending it all have crossed my mind a couple of times, but in God's mercy and grace He gave me a son so I could have a reason to stay alive and sane, even if only partially. I think what saved me to an extend as a child was that I used to seek escape from reality by reading, mainly fantasy and unrealistic love stories, or lying on the grass so I could look at the clouds changing shape while I daydream, and I loved watching movies, I still do.

But throughout the years, no matter what I did, I always felt immensely dissatisfied with my circumstances. Not only could I not find lasting inner peace, but I was miserable because I felt powerless to change my environment. I knew something was missing, but I did not yet have the knowledge on how to 'fix' it. I always believed in God, but I instinctively knew there was something more, something I was not told or did not yet know concerning faith.

I never thought myself to be a sensitive person, but I later realized my main struggle as a child and as a young person was due to the fact that I was highly sensitive, especially on a spiritual and emotional level. I was, and I am still to a large extent, unable to cope with the hardships in life. It scares me and causes me to withdraw. I am one of those people who wants to only experience love, peace and harmony, which seemed, for a very long time, to be only an illusion. I had to learn to seek for what I needed inside of me, there where God resides and where we are one.

I was unable to find solace in the Church because at first I thought I was unworthy and my imperfections reflected back at me, but later in life I realized I was unnecessary hard on myself. The church only consists of imperfect people, and if it was not for the grace and patience of God, everyone would be lost. I was constantly seeking for 'something else.' It felt to me that there had to be more. While still in Primary school I stood next to my dad one day while he was preparing a fire to roast meat. I looked up at the heavens and my heart cried out to God; 'Is this it? Is this what life is about? Eating, drinking, going to school and repeating the same routine day after day? God, surely there must be more, there has to be more, otherwise what is the point in living?'

It was only during my second marriage that I started reading inspiring, self-help books. I listened to tapes and watched the DVD's of many of the great teachers that are available, wonderful works that are there to help and guide a person in finding their true self, and by that, also inner peace. Some of the very first books I read were the works of the late Dr. Wayne W Dyer whom I greatly admire; 'Your sacred self, The power of intension and The Shift.' I also read the works of John Kehoe; 'Mind power into the 21st century,' and I did a Mind power course. Every time I read a self-help book or attended a workshop or seminar, I felt inspired to change my life. I would then decide that's it, I can do it, I can change my life, I can and will be happy! But alas, there are no short-cuts. No matter what I did, I still couldn't stop the constant, mindless, self-defeating chatter in my brain, or shake off the frequent episodes of depression, so I kept on seeking. I desired freedom; freedom to do what I want on my own terms and time, and above all I desired abundance!

I wanted lots and lots of money so I can do what I want, when I want – total freedom! I started reading, and listening to everything I could find my hands on. I made a study of how the brain functions, anything to help me on my path of finding inner peace and happiness, including everything on the law of attraction, making use of hypnosis and tapping, meditation, you name it, I have done it! Hay House is a useful source of information if you are seeking a spiritual path. The works of Dawn Clark was very helpful, but due to my impatient nature, I keep on 'moving on' in the hope of finding a lasting solution!

Guess what? The lasting solution I was seeking was me, or better; the Spirit of God in me! The 'I AM.' I know you have heard this before and maybe it didn't work for you because you did not understand how it's all linked together. You have to find inner peace irrespective of any and all outward circumstances. There will always be something that will 'pop up and attempt to steal your peace,' or so you will convince yourself, but it is still all you. You are allowing these peace-stealing-thieves into your life. As soon as one problem is resolved, another pops up. Why? Because you think that is what gives meaning to your life. It is your way of seeking your purpose – to justify your existence! When it's all smooth sailing, you get bored and start feeling useless, and to get the feeling of usefulness back you create the circumstances that will require some effort from your side so you can feel valuable again, something that will force you to use your skills.

Inner peace starts in your mind, and therefore you have to make an effort to obtain it irrespective of where in your journey you find yourself. You are able to do that because you were created to overcome adversity. A good way to start your journey to inner peace is through meditation. Keep on seeking, reading, declaring and practicing till you've reached your goal. Important; you have to do all of this while you're in a relaxed state of mind, because forcing the process will cause it to keep on eluding you. Without inner peace it will be difficult for you to claim your rightful place and own the space you occupy because you will continue to feel unworthy to do so!

Dr. Joe Dispenza says in his book called, 'Breaking the habit of being yourself,' the following, 'I know that it's frustrating when life seems to produce an endless succession of minor variations on the same negative outcomes. But as long as you stay the same person, as long as your electromagnetic signature remains the same, you can't expect a new outcome. To change your life is to change your energy - to make an elemental change in your mind and emotions. If you want a new outcome, you will have to break the habit of being yourself, and reinvent a *new* self.' Get it? You have to create a new version of your SELF. Nobody else can do it for you. Yes, with as much faith as a mustard seed you can move a mountain, but continual, lasting faith comes with practice. I do not yet see any mountains in the sea! Renewing *your* mind is something only you can do.

Someone once said in an article, 'If you were not trained as a child on how to make good choices and how to take responsibility for the consequences of the bad choices you make in your life, it will be difficult to understand the profound importance of making good choices. You often hear that everything is a choice, or that there is one thing we still own as humans, and that is the ability to choose, free will in other words, but nobody taught us how to use our free will wisely. If you believe, and take ownership of the fact that everything in your life happens because it is your will, even if it was an unconscious decision, you actually empower yourself, and if all children were taught this concept from a young age, I promise you, the world would be in a different place. No more blaming games. No more feelings of hopelessness, but rather well-balanced adults that take responsibility for their lives, and teach their children to be the same – euphoria!'

In his book, 'I can see clearly now,' Dr. Wayne W Dyer said the following, 'Every move I made in my life was in the direction of more freedom that gave me the ability to decide for myself where to be each day, what to wear, how to speak, how my writing would proceed. These were nudges from my soul—the inner invisible part of me that is infinite and therefore always seeking expansion. Stay in touch with and honor the calling you feel deep within you. Ignoring that will leave you feeling like a prisoner in your own body and in your own private world. Your soul is miserable when it is confined, or labelled, or told what it can or cannot do.'

My soul was miserable for a very long time. I ignored my inner voice for far too long due to the fact that I was scared and I did not believe I was good enough to receive anything good in this life. I was literally a prisoner in my own body.

A WORLD OF ABUNDANCE

We treasure our mortal lives, but it is a fleeting moment in time and space, the quiver of a feather in the wind before it gets blown away. A quiet mind is the first step to realizing the abundance in your life. By ignoring the constant chatter in your mind you'll be able to identify the truth from the lie. The lie will tell you that you have to constantly chase something to obtain more money, more possessions, more of everything. The thing is; when you chase, you have to keep on chasing. It never stops, but if you are content and thankful with what you have, but not lazy, and you trust divine guidance, what you have will increase. You first have to be happy with yourself - you must be content and accept and love yourself. You are abundance; you do not have to chase abundance. Think; what do you really need in your life to have the feeling of abundance? Do you believe that we live in a world of abundance, or in a world of lack?

We live in a world of plenty and everything around us is proof of that. Try and count the leaves on the trees in a forest, or the stars, or the sand on a beach (John Kehoe). Why can't you count it? Because there are too many, and that is called abundance! You are abundant, a creation of the most High – someone special, so why do we see so much lack, struggle and hardship in this world? Because we were never taught how to believe in ourselves, and we therefore do not know how to claim our rightful place or own the space we occupy. We are waiting for someone else to validate us - stop waiting!

Although we obviously live in a world of abundance, we are tricked into believing the opposite. If you grew up never hearing the words; 'No, it's not possible, there's no money, there is no food, no water,' or whatever negative words you were raised upon, you would expect things to be there when you need them to be. The enemy and other external forces have been brainwashing us for eons into a lacking mentality which causes fear and dependency on the systems of this world. Some call it the matrix. It is my personal believe that Christ was send to this earth to save us from the enemy and these external forces that is keeping us in mental and physical slavery so we can be free to live a life of abundance.

Jesus said in John 14:12-14, 'I tell you the solemn truth, the person who believes in me will perform the miraculous deeds that I am doing, and will perform greater deeds than these, because I am going to the Father. And I will do whatever you ask in my name, so that the Father may be glorified in the Son. If you ask me anything in my name, I will do it.' I can barely contain my excitement! Remember the faith like a mustard seed? Now combine the two. Ask in His name and have faith (do not doubt) that it shall be so – nothing will be impossible!

The worldly systems are currently under the control of the unseen world that was banished to earth and has mortal co-conspirators. I also believe that these mortal co-conspirators have been promised something that will not be delivered, but that they will only realize it when it's too late. Never in history has evil ever permanently prevailed over good, and it never will, even if it seems like it on the surface. We treasure our mortal lives, but it is a fleeting moment in time and space, the quiver of a feather in the wind before it gets blown away. Do not treasure your mortal lives too much; rather have eternity in mind when you make decisions about your future.

It seems all animal and plant-life on earth somehow, in what they do or the sounds (vibrations) they make, bring glory to the Creator, and I think humans also have that capability – it is our unique, individual frequency which we need to find. In finding our own 'ringtone' we will be in the right place at the right time all the time, in sync with creation, the universe and God. Abundance has to follow. Abundance is not only monetary; it is on all levels of life. Allow yourself to experience and enjoy a life of abundance.

MIND POWER

Mind power was and is God's idea, but the reason we are not aware of this truth is due to the fact that these types of ancient truths have been left out of the institutions that are supposed to educate its people. Doctrines have, over decades, been changed and in most cases only the basic themes – those ones that don't cause too much controversy so the masses can be kept happy and asleep, are taught. All scriptures are to our benefit. There are scriptures, if taught from infancy that will change your perception about yourself, life on this planet and your future. I believe there are ancient truths left out of the scriptures that we were supposed to be taught, like the fact that sound and vibration has a very powerful effect on a human being and that it even has the ability to cure many ailments. The ancient teaching of meditation has been withheld in most cultures over the world, and the results are obvious. The teaching of meditation is required to still our minds and teach us the fathomless love of God. Meditation should be an integral part of human existence; it is not to be regarded as something mystic. But don't despair; it's never too late to learn the truth.

Carefully consider the following words from Philippians 4:8, 'Whatever is true, whatever is worthy of respect, whatever is just, whatever is pure, whatever is lovely, whatever is commendable, if something is excellent or praiseworthy, think about these things.' The scripture says '*think* on these things,' that is mind power. Why must you think about these things? Because if you think these upstanding things every day you are setting yourself up for success and the enemy does not want that, because if you think doom and gloom every day, and if you are constantly negative and depressed, you are under his control. When you are miserable you are unable to claim your rightful place or own the space you occupy. Your vibrational signal is weak and you become non-existent – a non-threat!

I remind you of the following words that has the ability to change the world as we know it, 'I tell you the truth, if someone says to this mountain, 'Be lifted up and thrown into the sea,' and does not doubt in his heart but believes that what he says will happen, it will be done for him.' Mark 11:23. Imagine growing up with this ancient truth ringing in your ears day and night. With everyone believing in their own ability, and not doubting, the whole world would've looked much different than the one we are currently living in. Words are powerful, and so is your belief that something is true, because it will be true for you! Faith and having zero doubt that what you say will be so is the key here. We find more powerful words in the scriptures of the Bible which should be taught daily, here are a few:

'I tell you the truth, if you have faith the size of a mustard seed, you will say to this mountain, 'Move from here to there,' and it will move; nothing will be impossible for you.' Matthew 17:20. Wow! Nothing will be impossible? That is so profound!

'When the disciples saw it they were amazed, saying, 'How did the fig tree wither so quickly?' Jesus answered them, 'I tell you the truth, if you have faith and do not doubt, not only will you do what was done to the fig tree, but even if you say to this mountain, 'Be lifted up and thrown into the sea,' it will happen. And whatever you ask in prayer, if you believe, you will receive.' Matthew 21:20-22. I can hardly contain my excitement about this. It clearly shows proof of the law of attraction. If you ask and you believe (expect to receive) you will receive.

It is clear that God wants us to use 'mind power' in our daily lives. The idea that you should think positive thoughts, meditate on what is pure and wholesome and have faith to receive what you want is as old as time itself. We have to start using it in our lives and teach it to our children from a young age. Lucky for us God is alive and so is His Word (Jesus Christ), and it is possible for us to still learn from the Word (scriptures) the living words that keeps us spiritually alive. He has now imparted these truths onto the hearts of people He can trust to spread the word out into the world. There are wonderful teachers that have written books on the topics of mind power, self-empowerment and spiritual awakening. None of these topics excludes God, and know that it is not possible to separate the mind from the body because your mind influences your body. You can also not ignore your spirit, because without spiritual awakening you are bound to remain in submission to the physical world.

Here's another secret; everything in life can be learned, no matter what age you are. Your mind has the ability to adapt to change, and with repetition you are able to teach your mind and your body new habits since it's the habits you've learned over many years that is now running your life. Learning through repetition is how you are able to read, speak, and do everything else in your life – because you were taught! It is therefore possible to retrain yourself by using the same methods you used to learn how to speak, read, or ride a bicycle – through repetition, which is the same as practicing your new future EVERY day! Your age does not matter, trust me. And yes, it takes time - it does not happen overnight, but your progress is up to you. Are you willing to practice your new future every day? It is human nature to want to increase, as a matter of fact; God instructed the first humans to multiply and fill the earth. Increase is natural.

It is interesting that when we get used to achieving our goals by using mind power, we want more. We want to advance to a higher plane and achieve more. That is how the rich get richer. If you are a lazy person by nature then this is not for you, you need to be hungry for change and it is not going to fall in your lap. Choose to become more vigilant and choose to do something to change your life for the better. Nothing comes from nothing. Where there is no effort, there is no change. It is also important to know that most of the hundreds and thousands of thoughts that cross your mind every day are junk. It does not serve you in a positive way. You need to become more selective of which thoughts you want to accept and which ones not. The brain receives unwanted information on a daily and constant basis. You need to sift through them and disregard the thoughts that might have a negative impact on your life. There is no reason for you to believe that any thought is true.

'The Human Mind is a wonderful masterpiece that has immense potential. Most of its potentials, however, remain unused in most people, since it is not us who are in charge of things, but our Mind takes control of us. In order to control something, we first need to know the thing concerned - so, we must know our Mind so as to be in charge of it.' Frank M Wanderer (contributor to the Wake-up world.com website). There are a few important things we need to be aware of when it comes to our Mind. According to Frank M Wanderer, there are sixteen factors and he mentions it as follows:

- The most important thing we need to know about our Mind is that it is not something that exists separately, individually, like some inanimate object. The Mind is not an object – it is a process. The process of constantly streaming thoughts. This stream of thoughts is what we perceive as the 'Mind.' The very basic nature of thoughts is that they are in a constant move, and this motion, almost automatically, creates the Mind.

- A characteristic feature of our Mind is that it keeps roaming, wandering; it operates in something like an automatic mode. Thoughts come and go all the time.

- In most of our waking time, our Mind wanders either in the past or in the future, in our thoughts we deal with our experience of the past, offences we suffered in the past, or with our future plans, goals and fears.

- In most cases, our Mind is locked up in the prison of the past by an event the outcome of which is unpleasant to us. Our thoughts turn toward that event in the past, we would like do change the course of the events, or we worry what others might think of us because of our improper behavior in that past moment.

- Another way of becoming prisoners is when our Mind puts the spell of an imaginary future, or the image of a desired, idyllic state upon us. Then we mobilize all our energies to make those images come true, and we tend to pass by the opportunities offered by the present almost blindly.

- The creative force of the Mind is only accessible in the present moment, in the here and now.

- Our Mind is constantly evaluating things. It means that we do not simply live through our experiences, but we also categorize them as good or bad. We judge everything that happens to us and everybody we meet in our lives.

- Our Mind is constantly producing stories. The entirety of these stories comprises our personal histories.

- The Mind is usually rejecting of, or even hostile to, the present moment. We often think that this or that should not happen that way, I should be somewhere else now, in some much better place. Why do such things only happen to me all the time? Our mind is thus in a constant struggle with the present.

- The conditioned mental patterns of the Mind are realized as various systems of beliefs and patterns of thoughts in our lives.

- The conditioned mental patterns have been handed down to us by our parents, our community and the society in which we grow up, and we have also borrowed some from the media.

- We very often accept these ready-made mental patterns and beliefs uncritically, without any thinking; what is more, we identify with these patterns that will, in this way, be incorporated into our personalities.

- The conditioned mental patterns place the development of the Ego in the foreground, and make efforts to sustain that development until the end of the life of the individual. The programming supports the progress of the Ego, they urge us to develop a powerful and efficient Ego for ourselves, and they make us believe that it is the ultimate goal in human life.

- Our Mind itself deems our own mental image of our personal development good. At the same time, this half of the Mind deems the other half, the one we wish to change, bad. Mental images fight against each other, trying to overcome each other, using the weapons of selective perception and story fabrication.

- Our Mind is one of the most sophisticated, most complicated instruments in the world. In this modern, rushing world, however, the Mind is bombarded with information to the extent that it virtually overflows. On those occasions the amounts of unprocessed information whirl in the Mind so fast that we are sometimes afraid of going mad.

- The purpose of the Mind is to serve as a means of connections, to connect us to the world and to each other. Through the Mind, used with alert consciousness, creative energies are released to the world, and create a wonderful harmony there.

There is more than enough proof that changing your mind is necessary, and that it was and is God's idea right from the start. 'You were taught with reference to your former way of life to lay aside the old man who is being corrupted in accordance with deceitful desires, to be renewed in the spirit of your mind, and to put on the new man who has been created in God's image - in righteousness and holiness that comes from truth.' Ephesians 4:22-24.

The power of the mind is in the fact that it is possible to change, and by reading this book you are in the process of doing that. Mind power, or making use of the mind to create your future is possible because it was and is God's will for us to live the life we deserve - a life of abundance! By practicing your new future every day you will be able to claim your rightful place and own the space you occupy.

WHAT DO YOU BELIEVE?

Due to the fact that I've always preferred to be in control of situations, and anything less than being in control caused extreme discomfort in my mind, body and spirit, I was under the impression that I was actually in control of my life, but I wasn't. I only later realized that everything I believed and thought to be the truth were formed by my outer circumstances and what I've learned from my parents, in school, in church and every other environment I've ever came in contact with. That was a scary thought for me and I had to take a hard look at myself and my belief systems, especially the ones about my self-worth..

'Your actions and how you react towards circumstances that you think you have no control over is a clear indication of what your deep-seated belief systems are. These deep-seated belief systems will eventually find their form and materialize into your physical reality. As the saying goes, 'thoughts become things.' A few scattered thoughts are unlikely to manifest, but your true beliefs always does. It might be more accurate to say, 'beliefs become all things.' Nanice Ellis (contributor to Wake-up world.com). The result of this is that everything you were able to create thus far in your life was due to these subconscious beliefs. Nanice Ellis says further, 'When you understand how to use the law of belief, you have the power to create the life you desire. The problem is we have never been educated on how to consciously use the law of belief for our highest good.'

The law of belief is closely linked to the law of attraction and to what you sow, you will reap. Can you imagine how your life would've turned out if you were taught from a young age what the impacts of these laws were going to be in your life? Unfortunately, mostly due to ignorance, most people never received instruction on these ancient laws. It's however never too late to learn and to teach your own children.

I grew up with feelings of unworthiness, which in turn caused me to feel powerless and gave me a victim-mindset. It took a lot of unnecessary long, hard years for me to change that. Besides most parents enforcing these misguided feelings onto their children due to their own ignorance, the structure of most school systems further enforces the belief that our worth is linked to our performance; no performance - no worth. The feeling of unworthiness and powerlessness can cause severe depression, no matter what age you are. When children grow up with constant negative feelings about themselves, the road to recovery as an adult is always hard.

These incessant negative feelings eventually turns into hard-core belief systems that rules your life and make it close to impossible for you to claim your rightful place and own the space you occupy. It takes a huge effort to change wrong belief systems once they've become a part of your subconscious mind. The universe will meet you on your level of expectation, and if you believe that you do not deserve anything, that is exactly what you will get – nothing, and the circle of deception goes around and around, never ending in the truth, unless you break free from your wrong belief systems. It is possible, because 'all things are possible for the one who believes.' Mark 9:23. Your wrong belief systems, if untreated, will have an effect on your whole life – your future. It will poison every level of your existence and it will have an effect on your relationships, your finances, your health, and on how you raise your own children. That is a scary thought!

According to Nanice Ellis, 'the disempowering programs of unworthiness, powerlessness and victimhood are so prevalent in every aspect of our lives that we don't notice them anymore. On the other hand, once we learn to recognize them, everything becomes perfectly clear. In order for us to understand how these programs got installed in our psyches, we have to look at the systems and institutions that run our world:

- Educational Institution: installs the unworthiness program. From day one of school, we must pass tests and be evaluated for worth every step of the way.
- Criminal System: installs the victimhood program. The criminal system is set up, not to deter criminals, but rather to create them, perpetuating victimhood.
- Medical Institution: installs the powerlessness and victimhood programs, through the use of patient disempowerment.
- Religion: installs the powerlessness and unworthiness programs. Most religions teach people that something 'out there' has the power to choose their faith – with rewards for goodness and punishments for subjective sin.
- Government: installs the powerlessness program, where the people depend on their 'leaders' for laws and protection.

- War: installs programs of victimhood, powerless and unworthiness.
- Financial Institution: installs programs of unworthiness, powerlessness and victimhood.

Every one of these systems and institutions are designed to make us believe that we are powerless and at any moment we could be victimized. They program us to believe that our worth is dependent upon external sources and that we have to keep jumping through hoops in order to prove that we are worthy. Even when we feel worthy and powerful, there is always the fear that it can all be taken away – that at any moment we can lose everything through economic collapse, sickness or war. There is no mystery as to how, or why, humanity is enslaved – every aspect of society is set up to mentally imprison us by means of hi-jacking our belief system. We are in economic and environmental crisis because humanity is in a massive spiritual crisis.'

DOUBT, THE SILENT KILLER OF DREAMS AND ASPIRATIONS

One 'wrong' thought or word cannot cancel all your hard work. It is persistent wrong thinking and negative speaking that is the problem. There is however, one very sneaky thief that is able to steal your dreams and aspirations and kill all your hard work without you even realizing it, and that's called DOUBT. I call it the silent killer, because you are rarely aware of its influence in your life. Doubt sneaks into your thoughts without you noticing it. It is caused by your subconscious belief that you are not good enough and if you have not yet claimed your rightful place, doubt will forever be part of your thinking.

The definition of doubt is a feeling of uncertainty or lack of conviction, and the synonyms are unsureness, indecision, hesitation, apprehension, skepticism, distrust, unbelief. No matter how many times you declare your success, if you have as much doubt as the size of a mustard seed in your mind, it will cancel what you are trying to achieve. You have to find a way of cancelling out doubt by questioning doubt itself, for instance; when you get the feeling that you are experiencing doubt about what you want, ask yourself the question, 'Why am I doubting? Do I think I am not good enough?' When you bring doubt to your conscious thinking you can then say to yourself, 'Doubt is not real, it is only in my mind. I am worthy to receive whatever I want. There is no reason for me to think otherwise.'

By practicing your new future every day without fail you will be able to get rid of doubt to a large extend. It is normal to feel a small amount of doubt, but you cannot allow it to rule your life. Keep practicing, don't stop. You will naturally have days where it feels like everything is going downhill, but keep on reminding yourself that the bad feeling is only temporary.

THE ART OF LETTING GO

Letting go of what was and what could possibly be should be taught from a young age. It should be regarded as a crucial life skill and possibly also taught in schools, just to make sure everyone gets it. The inability to let go contributes to a huge part of our suffering. Letting go of all worries and fears are the key to inner peace, and without inner peace it is difficult to manifest your desires.

When you get used to thinking a certain way, or doing things a certain way, or just being busy all the time, it is difficult just to be. Letting go allows you to just be. When you let go, you are in a state of being and inner peace is achieved, which in turn allows you to manifest your desires. When you allow your mind to roam in the past or in the future or on what hurt you in the past, your mind gets restless and drives you nuts, or you get depressed. There are people who experienced very bad physical, emotional or spiritual hurts in their lives; some so bad I try not to think about it. I do not know anybody who did not go through some bad as a child, but it is different for each person.

You can however, claim back that which was stolen from you by claiming your rightful place and own the space you currently occupy. You must practice your new future every day. Get up and fight the spiritual fight because 'our struggle is not against flesh and blood, but against the rulers, against the powers, against the world rulers of this darkness, against the spiritual forces of evil in the heavens.' Ephesians 6:12.

Learn to switch off and just to be – to let go. Breathe deeply, become aware of your posture, and sit in a quiet spot to meditate. Your brain can sometimes act like a naughty child and throw tantrums, but you have to train it like you train a child. Listening to calming music or meditating has great benefit. When I feel agitated for some or other reason, I listen to music that is specifically designed to lift my vibrational energy. I remind myself daily that each passing moment belongs to the past and that I should try and remember only the things that makes me feel good about myself. We get bombarded with so many negative things on a daily basis that it becomes crucial to learn how to let go. Later in this book I discuss the 'Step into the Right-now-zone Method' that can be used as a tool to learn the art of letting go.

Zen Gardner, a contributor to the Wake-up world.com website says in his article titled; 'The time for letting go,' the following, 'That's the key. Detach from everything. We are the only ones who let anything have power over us. It happens when we're ignorant of the Truth and base our thoughts or actions on lies. It happens when we're tense, overly left brained about something, in a hurry, or many other 'reasons' - all to be vigilantly monitored and avoided. It happens when we try to defend ourselves and any sense of 'who we are.' It happens when wrong beliefs replace knowledge and experience. It happens when we don't respond to what Love tells us to do. It happens when we're attached to the outcome. This 'Velcro effect' is a tough one; it keeps growing back and catches so many. When we get set in our minds that something needs to be a certain way, or we need to be in a certain place, or at a certain time when it's actually arbitrary, or think our goals of any sort are 'set in stone,' we're setting ourselves up for trouble. That applies even more so to beliefs. What if the Universe opens another door? We're not free to enter it in that mindset. Our mind's made up. In fact, in that state of mind we can't even see the new door that's opened, for any one of the reasons listed above. In those states we're 'unconscious.'"

WHAT WORDS?

The sounds you utter, which are the words you speak, are alive. It has power because it carries vibration and vibration can move matter. Because you are a holistic entity with a body, mind and soul - a vibrational being with your own frequency which you emanate day and night, and your body consist of approximately 50 – 75% water - water has the ability to be influenced and to adapt to its surroundings, the words you speak and the words you listen to has an effect on your body, mind and spirit. Repeated thoughts and words becomes a habit and a habit becomes a belief. Belief systems run your life. Picture yourself as a vibrational being and see in your mind's eye how you emanate your frequency wherever you go while absorbing the frequencies of the people around you. Your frequency has a direct impact on the people around you, and vice versa.

What does this mean to you? How can this knowledge change your life? This means you have the power to influence your circumstances. You are able to change your future by the words you speak. It starts with a desire for change and the decision to start. Words first get their form in your mind before they leave your tongue, therefore teach yourself to first think on what you want or are about to say before you utter the words. It will be of great benefit to you. Remember, repetition is the key to learning everything unless you have a photographic memory. You will ultimately get out of life what you put in. You deserve to live the life you want, but it is difficult to attract the things you want when you vibrate the wrong frequency, and the words you speak has either a positive, or a negative influence on your vibration.

I believe that God is still communicating with us through words (vibration) and that the existing written Word, the Bible, are not His final words. I believe it is an ongoing thing. He is alive and we are alive and we are connected to Him and all other living things. We get revelation through our spirits and through our thoughts and through spoken, living words. I am convinced that the Holy Spirit inspires people till today to write down the words God wants to share with us. We have been blessed and inspired in this age with wonderful, spiritual teachers whose works are available for the ardent seeker of the higher meaning of life and self. We, as images of the Creator, has the ability to create with words, therefore you should choose your words wisely.

The best thing is that there is proof of the impact that words can have on us and on our environment. This proof was established by Masaru Emoto, a Japanese author, international researcher and entrepreneur who claimed that human consciousness has an effect on the molecular structure of water, and that water is the blueprint for our reality. You can view the full details and results of his research at: http://www.masaru-emoto.net/english/water-crystal.html.

In the words of PL Chang, 'Before we explore the magic power of words, I need to explain to you what magic is so you can see the relation between magic and the power of words. The term magic is derived from Old French *magique*, Latin *magicus*, and Greek *magikos*. One of the earliest definitions of magic is the 'art of influencing events and producing marvels using hidden natural forces. The Universe has many natural forces. Some of these forces are the engines that control the behavior of sound, light, vibration, and frequency. When you learn to use these forces to control energy, you can control how energy manifests itself into physical things to a significant degree. This is the art of magic. One way to tap into the magic power of words is to use the forces of thought, sound and sacred geometry. Sound plays a really important role for directing energy to create sacred geometries. These sacred geometric patterns are some of the building blocks of matter, which is why they can be found near the core of all material objects, even down to the level of atoms. The evidence proving that sound has the power to create sacred geometry can be seen in Cymatics (from Greek: κῦμα, meaning 'wave,' is a subset of modal vibrational phenomena).

A written word without sound is not that powerful. However, when you add sound to it by using your voice, the word vibrates with more energy and therefore becomes 'alive,' allowing it to do magical things. Because a spoken word has sound and sound can create sacred geometry, the right combination of spoken words can cast magic spells and control the flow of energy. Combine spoken words with the power of thought and emotion and certain natural elements (e.g., fire and water) and you have a very powerful tool to use for creating magic.'

As a matter of fact, that was how the creation of everything on this planet came about, through the vibration of the spoken word. Every time God created something, He SAID, 'Let there be,' or 'let the...' Genesis 1-2. There are so many things in this world that we do not yet understand. For me it is like opening one wrapped gift at a time and discovering something phenomenal inside! Make a decision today. Decide to start speaking only those living words into your life that will allow you to live a happy and prosperous life.

WHY DO WE TALK ABOUT HEALTH?

Health is not a topic I know much about, but I know that when my body is unwell, I feel miserable, and when I feel miserable my vibration is low and I am unable to cope with life since I am connected to my physical body. It is therefore of the outmost importance to stay as healthy as possible and to refrain from putting harmful substances in your body.

If you are not sure what you should eat or not eat, a simple guideline might help you to make better choices. Ask yourself, 'Is what I am about to eat natural?' If the answer is yes, then it will be a contribution to your body. However, still use the law of moderation. If the answer is no, then whatever you are about to eat is waste, because that is where it is going after you put your body through the process of using valuable energy to digest it, just so it can be filed under the 'useless, please discard' section. The bad thing is that unhealthy foods can make you feel miserable without you realizing that it's the food you ate that's responsible for your queasiness. You might eat something unhealthy now and feel great because it tasted good, but when you feel sluggish or bloated thirty to sixty minutes afterwards, you do not make the connection. You'll rather grab the anti-acid medicine instead. There is a sure connection between what you put in your mouth and how you feel physically. You can find a wealth of information and books on this subject at www.hayhouse.com.

Health is not only about food and the physical body, it is also spiritual. In her book 'Goddesses Never Age,' Christiane Northrup, M.D. says the following, 'The body is not uncivilized and in need of taming, but the vessel for our creative life force and the temple in which we're designed to live heaven on earth. When we recognize that we came here to live heaven on earth, we start to realize that our bodies are the only place in which we can do this. We stop denying our needs, start releasing the old emotional and physical toxins that have clogged up our energy centers, reclaim our energy and vitality, and awaken our inner healer. That's when the real magic happens, from reinventing our lives to rebooting our health.'

She also says further, 'The incredible inner healer in each of us is empowered by the ultimate healer; Divine Love (God). Working with this force, allowing it to fuel our lives is the key to healing our unhealed wounds. Asking Divine Love to take away our anger, sadness, and resentment over unhealed traumas of the past is the answer. It's only when we're awakened to our exquisite sensitivity and empathetic nature that we can acknowledge the need to heal. Pain in all its many forms - whether emotional or physical - is actually a most powerful path to Divine Love. Only a direct connection with the Divine will heal us permanently.' That is such a liberating way of looking at our health!

Dr. Wayne W Dyer had the following to say about health, 'So, what are your beliefs about what it takes to be in shape and physically healthy? Is it necessary for a person to suffer every day and go through a rigorous workout routine in order to be in good health physically? These are commonly held beliefs that should be challenged if you're seeking a more balanced life. Your wish is for a body that looks and feels terrific – that's the tenth rung desire. So what kind of thoughts do you entertain in order to reach this desire? All too often your thoughts go something like this: I'm not an active person. It doesn't matter how much I exercise - I still can't get the weight off and get in shape. I hate running and sweating. I'm not destined to be athletic. These beliefs, and many like them, keep you on the bottom rungs of that ladder. Moreover, they contribute enormously to the obesity crisis, and to the existence of so much lifestyle-related disease that originates in this kind of collective thinking.'

He says further, 'When you change your thoughts, and what you believe about what's possible for you, you change everything, including your physiology. You need to fervently believe that you're a specimen of perfect health by creating that picture of yourself as looking and feeling great. Carrying this image wherever you go and believing passionately in its reality is a total thought-changer! Now the inner dialogue will sound more like this: I'm heading in the direction of perfect health. I have no shame or guilt about myself or my behavior. If I choose to be a couch potato, I'll be a healthy, trim, beautiful couch potato. I love my body. I'm going to take great care of it because it houses the sacred being that I am. As you begin this new ritual of changing the way you look at your body, the body that you're looking at will change.' Wow! How liberating for all the couch potatoes out there. I know when I sit and watch television for more than one hour I start feeling immensely guilty and I imagine myself picking up weight.

Dr. Wayne W Dyer continues, 'You've been immersed in a culture that promotes how you should feel about your body, based on commercial endeavors that want to realize profits from your dissatisfaction with yourself. That sales pitch is that if you don't look like a supermodel, you should feel some remorse. Right there we have the beginnings of eating disorders, obesity, and weakened physical constitutions. When you buy into this kind of collective brainwashing, you set yourself up for a great imbalance between your desire to have a healthy body that feels great, and daily self-defeating behaviors leading to ill health and feeling exhausted and out of shape. Remember you become what you think about. Why think of yourself in any way that leads to less-than-perfect health? What's the point in looking at your body in its current condition of disrepair and taking on a set of beliefs guaranteed to make matters worse?'

These wise words of Wayne had a profound influence on how I changed my viewpoint about myself and my body. I think it is important not to succumb to the many opinions of the world on how you should look like, what is healthy, what you should eat and what not. You must, between all the guidelines available, decide for yourself. Be aware of what you ideal weight is and trust your instincts on how to reach it and on what you should eat to keep your body healthy. You instinctively know when you are eating the wrong foods, and it also makes you feel bad one way or the other. The symptoms will be there; it could be that you suddenly feel sluggish, or bloated, or you will have a headache, or a blocked nose, or you'll just feel ill. You will know. But if I can give any guidance, then this is it; everything from nature is good for your body; fresh fruits, vegetables, seeds and nuts, fresh meat, fish, chicken, but something that has been manufactured or processed in a factory could possibly be harmful to your body. There could be a few exceptions that I am not aware of.

It would've been fantastic if we were able to choose our own bodies, because if there's something we feel unhappy about when it comes to our outer shell, we tend to feel inadequate, and no matter how many people tell you that you are wonderful the way you are, you still wish you could change things. I, for instance, would've loved to be taller and have a wonderful, strong, olive-colored skin, but I don't. My question is therefore; why do we tend to look at other people and judge them on appearances if they were unable to choose how they look like? Isn't that a bit unfair?

When it comes to food, you are the only one that can choose what to eat or what not to eat. The power of everything in your life is in your hands. Taking care of your body is important and regular exercise will contribute to your overall feeling of well-being. When your body is out of shape, you're physical, emotional and spiritual vitalities are negatively affected - health does not only refer to your physical condition, it can also refer to your mental and psychological health which is equally, if not more, important. What good is there in being physically healthy but unable to enjoy it because your life is in such an emotional upheaval that it is affecting your psychological well-being? Our emotions also play a vital role in our mental and psychological health.

Carolanne Wright (contributor to the Wake-up world website) discusses the energy of emotions as follows: 'Leaders in the field of energetic medicine - including Sonia Choquette, Dr. Joe Dispenza, Dr. Bradley Nelson, Don Tolman, and others - explore the connection between emotions and offer active steps we can take to heal the body, the subconscious mind and our overall health. Taking into account the subconscious mind is 1000 times more powerful than the conscious mind we are likely to ask, 'What actually controls it?' The answer lies with unresolved emotions.

When we have traumatic perceptions buried in our subconscious mind, these emotional memories, when triggered, will cause a reaction in the body that sets off a cascade of stress hormones, thereby altering our physiology. How are these negative perceptions created? It is created by our thoughts, because thoughts create emotions. When we feel an emotion strongly enough, it will become trapped and disrupt the energy field of the body. Anger, aggression, anxiety, depression, sadness - these negative emotions will lodge themselves in the body and are the leading cause of physical pain. Eventually, if the blockage isn't cleared, disease will develop.

Dr. Joseph Mercola provides an example: 'Those suffering from depression will often experience chest pains, even when there's nothing physically wrong with their heart. Extreme grief can also have a devastating impact - not for nothing is the saying that someone 'died from a broken heart.' In the days after losing a loved one, your risk of suffering a heart attack shoots up by 21 times!' He also points out: 'Your body cannot tell the difference between an actual experience that triggers an emotional response, and an emotion fabricated through thought process alone - such as when worrying about something negative that might occur but has not actually happened, or conversely, thinking about something positive and pleasant. The fact that you can activate your body's stress response (which produces chemicals that can make you sick) simply by thinking means that you wield tremendous power over your physical state in every moment. Moreover, it means that you can literally manifest disease, or healing, by thinking.' Needless to say, in order to enjoy vibrant health, it's vitally important to release emotional baggage.'

Most people have issues with either some part of their bodies, their weight, or something else, but why? Because we are comparing ourselves with other people and we think we are falling short of the perfect image. 'When our actions come out of a place of feeling un-whole and lacking, we are fighting against a battle that can never be won and can only take us further down into a life-deteriorating path based upon something unreal. First of all, we need to notice in what way we have been socially conditioned to perceive ourselves as defective and unworthy. Start paying attention to the countless forces that are constantly bombarding you with fake pictures that portray the image of beauty, flawlessness, fitness and perfection. Then start noticing that way in which we are always offered a solution (usually in the form of something we must buy or consume) in order to fight against that which they made us believe we are lacking. Food, money and image have become agents of corporate greed. We must understand the paradigm of suffering that we've all inherited. The fuel of greed, vanity and power that most (not all) commercial products and socially rooted ideologies are based on, can lever lead us to our highest good.' Monica Rodriquez (contributor to the Wake-up world website).

The thing is, when you know who you are, and when you've managed to claim your rightful place and own the space you occupy, you will realize the triviality of the world's opinion on every level of your life. In the end, the only thing that will count is how you've lived your life.

THE AWAKENING

Ask yourself this question, 'Am I able to stand up for myself and firmly, but lovingly, insist that I be treated fairly? Am I able to take my rightful place and expect abundance in my life? Do I believe that I do not have to make an excuse for the fact that I exist because I am exactly where I'm supposed to be?'

If not, read on, but first make peace with the fact that lasting change happens slowly. It is impossible to change years and years of wrong input before and after birth, abuse, self-abuse, hate and self-hatred in one, or even two years. The most helpful information that opened my eyes and my mind was the truth that we are vibrational beings that receives and emanates vibration (frequency), and that sound has an integral effect on us, but more important than that, which is what I discovered through the Holy Spirit in me, is that we, each one of us, has our own unique frequency, as unique as our fingerprints, and unless you are ringing according to your own frequency, you will continue to feel out of place.

This makes it all worse, doesn't it? If it did not take me many years to come to this conclusion, I would've drowned this information out of my life due to pure frustration, and especially if I had to read this from someone else, because, HOW do you find your own frequency and change the wrong one you currently have? Could it be by claiming your rightful place and owning the space you occupy? Yes it is, but still, how do you DO that? It is forever the 'how' that eludes people.

First of all, stop giving your space and your place away to other people by getting out of the way for those whom you regard as 'better' than you. Nobody is better than you because there are only one you. You are also not above anyone else. Stand firm and fearlessly own your space and claim your rightful place. Secondly, refuse to be dictated to on how you should live your life. Stop comparing yourself to others. This is not an external battle, it is an internal decision. Begin to trust the Spirit of God, who is inside of you, to guide you in all things. God's Spirit can lead you into finding the frequency you should be ringing and the song you should be singing. You have to sing your own song! You should be free from the oppression of this world, and you are, but you must first wake up and realize that you are allowed to be free. Everything in life has a song and they sing it to the honor of the Creator. You too, have a frequency, and if you are not singing to your own tune, you have learned the song of another.

There is a little Japanese puffer fish that spends days creating a pattern which imitates (look like) a frequency on the ocean floor to attract a female – that's his way of contribution to the song of the universe! It does not matter if it is a cricket's song, a bird's song, or any other living being's song, although all different and beautiful in its own way, it is still the same glory to God. Certain binaural beats have the ability to trigger the release of endorphins. Why? Because we are vibration and we vibrate in fluid – water. Wake up to the knowledge that energy and vibration is what everything consists of.

Your spirit chose to be born and to have no knowledge of previous existence, which is the agreement you make when you leave the Creator's side to experience mortality, but you need to understand how things work – the forces at play, and the fact that we are in the center of it all. When you understand that you are in the middle of a battle, and you realize how things work and what you should do to claim your place, things start to change and you will gradually wake up. 'For our struggle is not against flesh and blood, but against the rulers, against the powers, against the world rulers of this darkness, against the spiritual forces of evil in the heavens.' Ephesians 6:12.

In the wise words of Zen Gardner, contributor to Wake-up world. com, 'When you become conscious - when you truly wake up, you realize you have nothing to defend, nothing to fear, nothing to strive for. You find out you're already complete and connected to everything. No one can take your freedom because you are freedom. You realize this whole game of life that's been meticulously laid out for us, is built upon implanted wants and perceived needs based on, amongst other things, a false sense of scarcity, and the impulse to strive to get what you are told you need. None of this has to be. It's all based on ignorance and the whims of a predator race that feeds off of the sleeping aphids they've co-created and manipulated. It is sad, but it's true. Letting go of this mindset is not an overnight thing, but your wake up can be. It takes time to realize all the ways we've been programmed and the vast quantity of disinformation and wrong mechanisms we've been given. The beautiful thing is it's actually a very simple process to get free. You just have to listen to your inner consciousness and dig into real and true information, then do what your awakened consciousness tells you to do. That's the catch - unless you put what you've learned to be true into action you'll be just another stillborn spiritual baby. That's not what you want.'

Change is both necessary and inevitable, but it starts with you and you alone. I know I am repeating myself, but nobody can make decisions on your behalf, only you can, even if you choose to follow the status quo, you are still the one making the choice, get it? This is how it works; there is no magic wand, and no one size fits all. Take the time to find out what works for you. Have patience in investigating everything and choose what works for you, but don't take too long to start learning how to meditate. It is more important than you think. Our biggest problem is our minds, and meditation will teach you how to discipline your mind and your thoughts. To me it seems that it is crucial to attain inner peace at any cost – that is the main aim.

I went through life with a burning desire to proof to myself and to the world that I am indeed worthy, which meant I ended up proclaiming, visualizing, repeating slogans and making vision boards for the money, the house, the car, all the stuff I thought will proof my worthiness to claim my rightful place in this world - things I thought would make me happy, but it was not working and I got more frustrated and depressed! Here's the thing; as long as you feel unworthy, none of the big material things will appear. You cannot lie to your own spirit. It knows what you really want and need and what you truly believe. Wealth is only a by-product of inner abundance.

I was forced to look inside myself and ask for inner guidance without forcing it. 'For everyone who asks receives, and the one who seeks finds, and to the one who knocks, the door will be opened.' Matthew 7:8. Because I persistently continued to ask and knock, it came to me; I had to ask God to lead me to the money, the house, the car, the relationship and circumstances that will really make me happy, those things that will keep me in the flow, energy and vibrational frequency that was meant for me - the physical, emotional and spiritual things that would bring me to a place of true fulfilment, without comparing myself to anyone else.

My daily prayer became the following; 'Thank you Lord for leading me to my true place of fulfilment, to my true home and true circumstances that you know will bring me peace and happiness. Thank you for guiding me toward that which my heart knows I truly need. Amen.'

Waking up is a process and you owe it to yourself to find a way, but it must be your awakening, not your awakening based on what others dictate. Start today. You can make use of the material that Hay House (www.hayhouse.com) has to offer. Hay House has some of the best tools and teachers to help you on your journey to change and fulfilment. Find the tool and teacher that fits you. I started with the works of Dr. Wayne W Dyer.

Some ardent seekers of the truth are of the meaning that we are dreaming and that waking up in our dream is the real secret to manifestation. For newcomers to this concept it might appear outlandish, but keep an open mind and take from it only that which will benefit you on the path where you are now.

Nanice Ellis (contributor to the Wake-up world.com website) says the following, 'We are dreaming and nothing is happening outside of us. That means that there is no competition and nothing that you cannot be, do or have. This is your dream and you are the dreamer.

Indeed, this can be a scary realization or the most liberated. Don't let the real in 'reality' fool you. It is all just smoke and mirrors disguised as a flowing and logical story that the human mind can project, process and accept as real. If you could step back for just a moment, you would clearly see that when you withdraw your energetic and emotional participation, the 'state of reality' melts away as the dream. This is the beginning of spiritual awakening. This is the beginning of true freedom and liberation from perceived bondage. After all, how can you be imprisoned in a dream?'

Waking up is a process, but you owe it to yourself to keep on seeking till you have reached your goal. We were not born to be slaves of the systems of the world. We were created to be the rulers on this earth. Know that you are worthy, and that you do not have to earn your worthiness in some way or justify your existence.

TIME IS OF NO CONSEQUENCE

Something profound happened to me in the early hours of 14 June 2016; I dreamt, rather experienced (because it felt as if I was present in the flesh) that I was able to see how scared, lonely and emotional my mother was while carrying me in her womb. The month of June is two months before my birth date on the 7th of August. I could feel how her emotions affected me and how tense and scared I was in her womb. It was like I was under attack! It was horrible. She was crying, and so was I. Afterwards I knew that was the reason why I always had a tendency to become over-emotional, and I used to cry easily.

In my dream I started talking to my unborn self. I used calming, soothing words and I told myself everything was going to be okay, and that I love myself. I could literally feel my baby self calming down in my mother's womb. When I woke up, it felt like a heavy mountain was lifted from my soul. Even when I thought about the incident afterwards, I had no desire to cry, which was new for me, since I used to be a real cry-baby when I engaged in thoughts about my childhood! A new feeling of freedom was released in my core – what an experience!

For a few days after the dream I deliberately took time to imagine myself as a baby while I talk to myself, reassuring my baby self that everything was okay and that I love her. Every time I could sense change happening in my core, so I kept at it for a couple of days. It was as if time was of no consequence. In these sessions I also spoke to my mother. I told her that I love her and that everything would be okay. I could literally feel her calming down every time I did it. I think there is a lot in life we do not yet know or understand, especially about time - I can't wait to get to know all of that which is hidden.

FEAR AND THE VICTIM-MINDSET

I cannot mention the word fear without thinking of the word paralyze, because fear has the ability to paralyze mind, body and soul. The definition for fear is: an unpleasant emotion caused by the belief that someone or something is dangerous, likely to cause pain, or a threat. The synonyms for fear are: terror, fright, fearfulness, horror, alarm, panic, agitation, trepidation, dread, consternation.

The definition for paralyze is: cause (a person or part of the body) to become partly or wholly incapable of movement. The synonyms for paralyze are: disable, cripple, immobilize, incapacitate, debilitate. Can you see that fear has the ability to disable and cripple you on a physical, emotional and spiritual level? Fear is a scary word because of its meaning, but more so because of what it can do. It can shut you down like a virus can shut down a whole computer system.

Fear has the ability to stop you from finding your true self and stop you from claiming your rightful place and owning the space you occupy, it can cause you to become an empty vessel without a purpose. Fear can also cause you to cultivate a victim-mindset, and as long as you have a victim-mindset, you will never be free from oppression. Fear sets in motion a chain reaction of negative thoughts, feelings and emotions that ends up in depression, which in turn, can make you physically, emotionally and spiritually sick. Did you know fear can have such a devastating effect on you and on your life? Well, what to do about it? How do you conquer fear?

According to Brene Brown, a researcher at the University of Houston, Graduate School of Social Work, the belief in our own unworthiness drives us to live fear-based lives. We are afraid of letting people see who we really are and potentially exposing ourselves. She further said that to conquer our fear we must 'dare greatly,' or go out there in the arena and expose ourselves to failure and criticism.

'There is no fear in love. But perfect love drives out fear, because fear has to do with punishment. The one who fears is not made perfect in love.' 1 John 4:18. What should this mean to you and how do you apply it? According to this scripture fear for something or fear to do something is caused by the fear of getting punished or hurt in some way, for instance; if you fear to try something different you might link it to the fear of failure as some sort of punishment, and if you fear to jump over a big hole in the ground it could be linked to the fear you have of getting hurt, which can be seen as some sort of punishment. But love conquers all, and I think fear should be resisted like we have to resist the enemy. It is said that if you resist the enemy he will flee from you, and I have come to realize that if you first acknowledge fear and thereby exposing it, and then resist it though courage, it tends to flee from you. Doing something even if you fear doing it is called courage. Aristotle believed courage to be the most important quality in a man. He said courage is the first of human virtues because it makes all other virtues possible.

It is logical that you will not do something that will put your life in danger. There is something like healthy fear. You will not put your hand out to pet a wild tiger. You might end up as his dinner. Be wise and act with foresight. When you allow the paralyzing effects of fear for too long in your life, depression can set in, and depression is a very dangerous, but curable disease. I struggled with depression for a very long time and I therefore am aware of its devastating influence on mind, body and soul.

'If life is meant to be joyful, why are we faced with a global pandemic of depression?' Nanice Ellis. A feeling of powerlessness is a great cause of depression. When you feel you have no control over what happens to you, it causes a feeling of despondency where you cannot see a way out of your problems, and that in turn causes depression. Since we were supposed to rule, each on our own piece of land, and life did not turn out like that for many people, a greater sense of worthlessness is prevailing. Some people do not even have a home. The feeling of

CLAIM YOUR RIGHTFUL PLACE

worthlessness can be greater for men since they are supposed to be the rulers of their own kingdoms – their homes and families. When a man has no kingdom to rule over, it might feel to him as if he has no identity! There is true liberation in waking up to the truth that we are in control of our own lives and that people make man-made rules, and we are the people! You are supposed to adhere to God's laws and the rules of a land, but you are free to govern yourself.

'We need to wake-up and stop following antiquated rules and programs that are intended to brainwash us to play unconscious roles in controlling those who look up to us and trust us. The broken system runs because we sustain it. Unsustainable systems eventually collapse. As long as we seek external solutions to our problems and blame those who seem to be in control, we will never realize that it is our beliefs that project, create and attract the reality that we experience. The external chaos is a manifestation of your beliefs, and keeps you from finding the real cause of issues which lies within you, in the form of your own beliefs. You have the absolute power to consciously create your life and no one can ever control you or manipulate your reality, unless you allow them. It is easy to give away your power when you are asleep but impossible for anyone to take your power when you are awake. You don't have to overcome depression – you just have to wake up. The opposite of depressed is awakened. This truth shall set you free.' Nanice Ellis.

There is no need to physically fight a battle for you to win your power back. You have already read that our fight is not in the physical realm, but in the spiritual realm, therefore our weapons are not physical, but spiritual. Realizing you have the power in your hands, especially in your mind, is your first spiritual weapon. Arm yourself with the right ammunition – believe in yourself, and believe in God. Claim your rightful place on this earth and own the space you occupy. You owe it to yourself and your descendants.

'This is not a war – this is an awakening. We are talking about taking our power back through a total rebellion of the mind. In order to emancipate ourselves from mental slavery we must reclaim our beliefs. We must turn off those obnoxious disempowering programs that have been running us and our ancestors for countless centuries — maybe even longer.' Nancine Ellis

Fear and a feeling of unworthiness and powerlessness can cause a victim-mindset, which in turn can prevent you from waking up and realizing that you are the one in control, but do not allow despair to enter your heart, rather continue to claim your rightful place and practice your new future every day, and you WILL reach your place of victory!

ALLOW LOVE

ALLOW YOURSELF TO BE LOVED

This was always the most difficult thing for me to do – to allow myself to be loved. I never felt I was worthy of anything. It's really crazy to think anybody can have such a low self-esteem and still exist. I caught myself red handed on numerous occasions; pulling away, causing a fight the minute a person tell me that they love me. I do not know why I was unable to believe that I am worthy of love and why I did not want to allow anyone close to me. It spilled over on all levels of my existence; physical, spiritual and emotional.

I had to ask myself if it was possible that there might've been a deeper, possibly unconscious reason for me to feel so negative about myself. I even went as far as investigating the possibility of being physically abused as a child, but there was nothing of that sort. Although my parents were neglectful in a huge way I do believe that they loved us (me and my siblings) in their own way. Like any other teenager, I was rebellious and wanted to run away, but it still did not explain the deep level of unworthy feelings I had about myself and why it was always difficult for me to allow anyone close to me.

I had to teach myself to be loved. I had to first comprehend that without other people my existence does not have meaning. I was always first to declare that I wanted to be alone, all by myself on a deserted island, but it does not work that way. You and I were created to be with other people. Your family and friends are precious, so look after them, cherish the time you spend together, even if they drive you crazy.

LOVE THY SELF!

It sounds easy enough; love thy self, but it is not easy. Some people tend to be very critical of themselves, even to the brink of self-loathing. I am sure it's not applicable to all people, but on one level or another, everyone compares themselves with others. It is easy to self-criticize and most people fall victim to it.

In the words of Dr. Wayne D Dyer, 'If you're not receiving the love you desire, it seems like a pretty good idea to explore what's creating this state. Obviously, most of us want to place the blame for lovelessness on something external to ourselves. That's a waste of time and energy, but it often feels good because blame seems to alleviate the pain, even if only briefly. However, blame energy only helps you remain out of balance, whether you're blaming yourself or someone else. Being in balance is centered on the premise that you receive in life what you're aligned with.'

There are a few guidelines that can help you in your quest of loving yourself. It is found in 1 Corinthians 13:4-7 which says, 'Love is patient, love is kind, it is not envious. Love does not brag, it is not puffed up. It is not rude, it is not self-serving, it is not easily angered or resentful. It is not glad about injustice, but rejoices in the truth.

It bears all things, believes all things, hopes all things, endure all things.' You can learn to love yourself by starting to apply some of these attributes to your life, like patience and kindness. Be patient and kind to yourself. Loving yourself will eventually spill over to others, which is the ultimate goal. Galatians 5:14, 'For the whole law can be summed up in a single commandment, namely, 'You must love your neighbour as yourself.'

Dr. Wayne D Dyer said further, 'While you may justify your loveless state with thoughts of being unappreciated, or choose to see the whole world as an unloving place, the fact remains that you're experiencing the imbalance of not feeling good because you don't have enough love in your life. Waiting for others to change, or for some kind of shift to take place in the world to restore you to balance, won't work without your commitment to take responsibility for changing your way of thinking. If that's left to others, you'll turn the controls of your life over to someone or something outside of you. And that's a prescription for disaster. The point I want to emphasize here is that if feelings of being short-changed in the love dimension are a part of your life, then it's because you've aligned your thoughts and behaviors with lovelessness. To balance your life with more lovingness, you need to match your thoughts and behaviors with those of your Source, being love in the way that God is.'

I cannot stress the importance of accepting and loving yourself enough. Without self-love it will be impossible to claim your rightful place or own the space you occupy, because you will continue to think everyone else is better than you and you will cede your rightful place to those you think deserve it more than you.

ALLOW LIFE TO HAPPEN

While driving over Sir Lowry's Pass, Western Cape, on my way to work one morning it hit me as I was watching the beautiful mountains and the calm sea in the distance while listening to a Michael Jackson song, that I was actually questioning myself if I should be enjoying this song, and then the realization hit me even harder; this is what I've been doing my whole life, with everything! I was constantly questioning if I should be doing this or enjoying that – and that was my problem! I was not allowing life to happen to me. I was waiting for everything to be perfect before I could actually enjoy it, but it was never perfect and it is never going to be. Who cares about the rumors that Michael Jackson had drug problems, or that he was accused of nearly dropping his child from a balcony? He was a fantastic artist, off course I was allowed to enjoy his music!

It is okay to love life, and to enjoy everything! Oh. My. Gosh! I have been depriving myself of life itself, and it took me more than fifty years to realize that, but it's not too late, it's never too late to fix something, unless you are dead. You should allow yourself to live life to the fullest, and enjoy every moment. Allow yourself to have the home of your dreams, the car, the boat, the relationships, or whatever it is you think will make you happy. Granted; material things alone cannot give you lasting happiness, but it does give you a sense of accomplishment which I think is important. I had to realize that it was me who was blocking all the wonderful things in life from happening to me because I was scared of life itself.

I eventually reached a point where I had to ask myself the following;

'If I was able to literally create a world, how would it be to live in that world? And if I was the only example that could be followed, what type of example would I set?' This made me realize that I was not allowing myself to live the life I really wanted, because I was limiting myself!

SELF-AWARENESS AND CALM

Becoming aware of your inner self and believing in your own self-worth is imperative to the wellbeing of all humanity. Digging deep in the inner-most recesses of your being to conjure up a calm spirit while everything around you is raging out of control is becoming one of the outmost important things you will be able to do to enable your mental and spiritual survival. It is proven that meditation can assist you in training your brain to behave. Our minds tend to carry on like naughty, hyperactive children, roaming around with thoughts that are not always to our benefit. The past, present, future and all kinds of worries and fears keeps our minds busy, but with meditation you will learn to discipline your mind.

In the words of Tania Kotsos, 'Meditation is the single most powerful technique that you can use to raise your degree of consciousness so as to consciously direct your life. Ultimately, you may have all the knowledge in the world but if you do not apply it through meditation, its usefulness is greatly diminished; yet few people truly know how to meditate. Some people are aware of what I call the depth of meditation, which is to enter deep states of mental and bodily relaxation for some purpose. But it is at the height of meditation that you will discover the mighty I within.

And it is only from this higher state of consciousness that you can truly become the director of your life.'

I think it is also important to allow yourself the time to do nothing. Doing nothing is just as important as doing something. We need time to relax; it helps our creative juices to flow. In your state of 'nothingness' you should have a pen and notebook at hand, because the insights you receive at that moment can steer your life in the direction it should go.

Realizing that you are actually the person in control of your life and that you have certain rights can have a calming effect on your mind. When you are taken into custody by the police, for instance, they have to read you your rights; 'you have the right to remain silent and you have the right to legal representation,' but when you realize that you have more rights than that in life, calm takes hold of you. You have the right to say no to things that does not suit you, the right to live the life you want, your way. You do not have to conform to society's rules, except the rules and regulations required by your government and the moral laws set out by God, other than that you should be your own person. People make rules, people can change them. You are the people! It is possible to be assertive without being arrogant, as a matter of fact; some of the most successful people in life are humble people.

We must understand that due to what happened in the beginning of creation, we are trapped in our minds and our brains has a sort of veil over it that mostly renders us incapable of perceiving other dimensions or become self-aware. It does not mean that if we cannot see other dimensions it does not exist. We are living with some sort of brain fog and it gets incited by our bad eating habits; what we put into our mouths has an effect on our bodies and our brains, and it gets further provoked by all the other distractions that life offers, not excluding television and the other trivial things we have to execute to stay alive in our daily lives. It's like we forgot who we are and where we are and we tend to tire quickly because of all the outside interferences. This lack of focus puts us into a deep spiritual slumber.

It is difficult to wake up, but we must be vigilant. Tell yourself daily that you are sleeping and that you are in a dream and should wake up. Do it as regularly as possible. Keep on reminding yourself that our fight is not physical, but spiritual, and it was brought on by what happened between the first humans and the enemy in the Garden of Eden. Become aware of your habitual thoughts and how you feel about everything around you, even something as uneventful as drinking a glass of water. Make sure you express appreciation, or utter a blessing for everything you are able to achieve, no matter how small. You can either think it or speak the words of appreciation out loud; it does not matter since everything has a vibrational frequency and has an impact on the things outside of you. Self-awareness will help you to take back what is yours - to claim your rightful place and to own the space you occupy, not by brute force, but by applying the mental and spiritual powers which we all have.

REFUSE TO GIVE UP!

You must become the best version of who you are, not according to anybody else, and giving up is not an option.

It felt like I've spent most of my precious time on this earth striving to become someone else while in constant turmoil and unhappiness.

I've been struggling to get the upper hand on creating my own life and restoring inner peace and calm and to break free from the unseen bonds that were holding me captive for a very long time. Why was I struggling so much? Because I first had to come to the realization that I already have everything inside of me; my abundance, my freedom, good relationships, everything, and that I cannot do it without God and His Spirit in me. I had to accept the fact that everything in my life was my own doing. It's like I have written the script and created the characters. I was directing every scene!

Another aspect that kept me in my own prison was fear. I was scared of life itself. It rendered me unproductive and powerless. I was in constant conflict with myself. On the one side I wanted to be free, but on the other side I was too scared to wander out of my comfort zone. This meant I had to force myself to cultivate bravery and courage by doing exactly that which I was afraid of. I had to stop second-guessing myself and have confidence that what I thought, decided and planned was the right thing to do. I had to sift my thoughts and eliminate the ones that did not serve me.

More important than all of this was to never give up - I refused to give up on my dreams. At first it was hard, but as I pushed the boundaries further and further, it became easier. I then decided to practice my new future every day and bit by bit, I started to claim back my rightful place. You should be able to dance with everything in you to the music you love.

Feeling disappointed or downhearted is a natural phenomenal, but you have to practice getting over bad feelings and emotions. When you continue to cherish bad thoughts and habits, it will materialize into all different kinds of monsters in your life. Repetition is the key to learning everything, it is therefore important to keep on practicing your new future every day. Allow love, allow life, and refuse to give up until you've reached your goal!

PRACTICE YOUR NEW FUTURE EVERY DAY

There is more to life than what you've been told. That's the good news. I would die if someone was able to convince me that life was only about eating, drinking, working and sleeping - so mundane. If you want to change your life permanently you MUST get off autopilot and practice your new future every day. Practice makes perfect is an age-old saying, but it is true. By practicing your new future every day you will be able to claim your rightful place and own the space you occupy. You have to discover who you really are, how your mind works, how you can use it to benefit you and change your life for the better by creating a new reality, and how to connect to your inner self, everything in the universe, and God.

In the beginning your mind will resist the change because it thinks it has to protect you from the unknown, whom it sees as a threat, but gently persist and allow yourself to get use to the idea of practicing your new future every day till you have reached your goal. It is said that in average, it takes twenty-one days for your mind to get used to a new idea, but you must persist past the twenty-one days if that is what it takes. You have to persist in developing new habits - your new future depends on it. Allow space for bad days and days where you will feel discouraged by letting go of the need to manage and control everything in your life. Total surrender is the perfect place to be, and the hardest place to find.

In my own journey, I came to realize that there are specific reasons why I get to the point of feeling discouraged. Here they are:

- When I feel I am not accomplishing my goals, or not accomplishing them fast enough.
- When my personal relationships with other people are in disharmony.
- When I feel alone, unloved or not worthy.
- When I sleep too little, or too much.
- When I eat unhealthy foods.

These are all things that can be overcome by making yourself aware that they exist, and by putting methods in place to prevent them from happening. When you go through a quiet time in your life where you feel nothing is happening, you still have to believe that things are lining up to your benefit, even if it takes longer than you anticipated - keep the faith.

What does it mean to practice your new future every day? It means that you first get to decide how you want your life to be, and then you do whatever it takes to reach that goal. The world is waking up to this wonderful knowledge; that you can create your circumstances through your thoughts. Pure thoughts attract good things into your life while evil thoughts will attract negative things into your life. The law of sow and reap – law of attraction, is as unyielding as the law of gravity, yet everybody seems to accept the law of gravity but negates the law of sow and reap. You are able to choose the thoughts, words and feelings that are in line with the future you desire. You are able to practice these new thoughts, words and feelings until you live the life you want.

WHO ARE YOU?

You are a holistic entity with a body, mind and soul, a vibrational being with your own frequency which you emanate day and night. How can this knowledge change your life? The fact that you are broadcasting your frequency out into the world constantly means you are able to influence your circumstances. By applying the knowledge you acquired in regards to what you think and speak, you will be able to find your own identity, which is the frequency that you should be vibrating (broadcasting). When you find your individual frequency, you will be able to truly exercise your birthright by claiming your rightful place and owning the space you occupy. You are able to change your future. It starts with a desire for change, and the decision to start. You ultimately get out of life what you put in.

When there is doubt in your heart, or if you are unsure of yourself, it is like a picture that is out of focus, you are distorted and your vibrational frequency is unclear. I tend to think that causes the universe not to recognize you – it does not see you, and therefore cannot grant your wishes, but, if your vibration is strong, and I can imagine that it becomes strong by believing in yourself, the universe will grant your requests by saying; 'Oh, there you are, I did not see you before. There you go, your wish is granted.' When you pray, for instance, you believe, and when you believe, your vibration is strong and that is why prayers are answered.

Dr. Joe Dispenza says in his book, Breaking the habit of being yourself, 'If your intentions and desires haven't produced consistent results, you've probably been sending an incoherent, mixed message into the field. You may want wealth, you may think 'wealthy' thoughts, but if you *feel* poor, you aren't going to attract financial abundance to yourself. Why not? Because thoughts are the language of the brain, and feelings are the language of the body. You're thinking one way and feeling another way. And when the mind is in opposition to the body (or vice versa), the field won't respond in any consistent way. Instead, when mind and body are working together, when our thoughts and feelings are aligned, when we are in a new state of being, then we are sending a coherent signal on the airwaves of the invisible.'

As I suggested before in my discussion under the heading; 'What words,' picture yourself as a vibrational being, emanating frequency wherever you go and absorbing the frequencies around you. Your frequency has a direct impact on the people around you, and vice versa due to the fact that you, and every living creature on this planet, consist mainly of water. Proof of the impact your vibrational frequency have on yourself and everything around you through water was established by Masaru Emoto, a Japanese author, international researcher and entrepreneur, who claimed that human consciousness has an effect on the molecular structure of water, and that water is the blueprint for our reality.

Some of the results done on frozen water molecules were astounding. The molecules that were exposed to a negative vibration that represented a negative word or emotion like, 'you fool,' or 'you disgust me,' showed clear indications of distortion and ugliness. The frozen water molecules that were exposed to positive words and emotions, representing a positive vibration like 'thank you,' or 'love and gratitude,' formed beautiful, well-formed crystals. These images can be seen at: http://www.masaru-emoto.net/english/water-crystal.html.

You and I are made mainly out of water and other fluids. Imagine the impact your negative words and emotions have on the people around you. A spoken word emanates vibration, and that is the reason for its power and why music has the ability to influence us on a physical, spiritual and emotional level. Your thoughts and feelings also emanate a frequency, and therefore have the same power as the spoken word. Everything you say, think and feel has an influence on your physical, spiritual and emotional wellbeing. By vibrating at a certain frequency, you unconsciously attract circumstances to match your current frequency. Therefore, if you want to attract different circumstances, you will have to change your frequency.

'Vibration is our unique personal energy frequency, or energy signature. It is the state of our energy at this moment as a result of all beliefs, emotions, experiences and interactions we have accumulated. Our vibration is directly affected by both the external such as our environmental factors and lifestyle choices, as well as the internal such as our thoughts and beliefs. Hence, it is essential for us to take care of ourselves on the physical, emotional, mental and spiritual levels to maintain high vibration.' Juliet Tang (contributor to Wake-up World.com).

RAISE YOUR VIBRATIONAL FREQUENCY

Negative thoughts and emotions vibrate on a lower frequency than positive thoughts and emotions. The key is to become aware of your current vibrational frequency and raise it. Just like everything else in life that gets mastered by practice, lifting your vibration to change your frequency will become part of who you are. It will become a habit. I make use of self-motivation/self-talk. The minute I recognize that I am vibrating on a lower level, I start talking (or thinking) to myself. I start by telling myself things like, 'I love you, Madeleen,' or when I'm worried about something, I will deliberately tell myself that there is no proof that what I am thinking is the truth.

Examples of low frequency thoughts and emotions

- Being sad
- Depressed
- Low self-esteem
- Doubtful (uncertain)
- Sickness (ill health)
- Negativity
- Anger
- Fearfulness
- Hateful
- Feelings of apathy
- Frustration
- Judgement of self and others

Examples of high frequency thoughts and emotions:

- Feelings of happiness
- Peaceful
- Positive
- Certainty
- Friendliness
- Hospitable (generous)
- Kindness
- Joy
- Love
- Good health
- Feelings of abundance
- Self-acceptance
- Self-confidence
- Forgiving self and others

It is possible to raise your vibrational frequency by speaking, thinking and feeling the opposite of the things on the list of examples of low frequency thoughts and emotions. We have established earlier in this book that your thoughts are not necessarily true or even your own and you therefore have the ability to choose which thoughts serve you and which ones not. That means you can change a thought or deliberately replace a negative thought with a positive one.

'Everything is vibration, from the highest mountain, to the smallest raindrop, including you. You don't see things as vibration because you are an unconscious expert at interpreting vibration into what you call reality. It is your inner interpretation that makes everything seems solid, but that is an illusion. This is great news because it means that you don't have to wrestle solid things to the ground to overcome them, nor do you have to change reality by force. It means that you only need to change your vibration in order to evolve yourself and the world, and that the transformation of humanity is simply a vibratory shift to higher frequencies. There is nothing more important than how you are vibrating. Your personal vibration is your greatest resource and more vital than money, time or even physical energy. Everything is second to your vibration. When you vibrate on a low frequency, life is difficult and relationships are challenging. Scarcity is often the norm and you spend your life trying to get by and survive.' Nancine Ellis.

A CRAZY PARADOX

The vibrational frequency of abundance begets abundance; therefore you cannot attract abundance from the vibrational frequency of lack. So the question is; how can you vibrate the higher frequency of abundance if you're in a situation of lack? This is where gratitude steps in. By practicing feelings of gratitude, even for the little you have, you are raising your vibrational frequency. The secret is to keep practicing gratitude. Remember, you are practicing your new future every day! Don't give up!

WHAT IS SHAPING YOUR FUTURE?

'You have the power to become anything that you want. Set your expectations for yourself, and know that you will become whatever you think about.' Dr. Wayne W Dyer.

Based on what you read so far, it is safe to say that your thoughts, words, feelings, beliefs and actions shape your future due to the fact that your whole being, and everything you do emanates a vibration that has a direct effect on you and the people around you. That means you can stop blaming God, other people, or your circumstances for your life. If you don't like your current life and circumstances, you have the power to change it. You are in control. Nobody can change your mind or make a decision for yourself but yourself.

HOW DOES YOUR MIND REALLY WORK?

Your mind consists of the conscious, subconscious, and the unconscious mind. Each has its own function. When you understand how they work together as separate entities, it helps you to consciously change thoughts that do not help shape the future you want and deserve.

According to the Mind Unleashed website, 'the concept of three levels of mind was nothing new. Sigmund Freud, the famous Austrian psychologist was the first to popularize it into mainstream society as we know it today. Even though his theories have subsequently been widely disputed in Psychology circles because they are very hard to scientifically prove, Freud nonetheless created a useful model of the mind, which he separated into three tiers or sections – the conscious, subconscious, and unconscious mind.'

Your conscious mind is the mind you use when you are consciously aware of your surroundings. It has the ability to direct your focus and to imagine that which is not real. The other important ability of the conscious mind is the use of visualization. Your mind can literally imagine something that is totally new and unique – something you've never physically experienced before. By contrast, your subconscious can only offer versions of what memories it has stored of your past experiences. You use your conscious mind when you are awake and have to make decisions based on what you see in the physical world.

Your subconscious mind is the work desk of your mind. Its job is to hold the programs and data that are currently in use so they can be reached quickly and easily and it is able to obey orders. It can't distinguish between that which the conscious mind imagines and that which is real, so whatever is brought up by conscious imagination and intently focused on, also brings up all the emotions and feelings that are associated with that image in your mind for you to experience. It works hard at ensuring that you have everything you need for quick recall and access when you need it. Things like memories, such as what your telephone number is, how to drive a car without having to consciously think about it, what you need to get from the shop, etc. Programs you run daily, such as behaviors, habits, moods. It filters your beliefs and values to test the validity of the information you receive daily. It receives sensations taken in via your five senses, and what it means to you.

Your unconscious mind is the storage place for all your memories that have been repressed or which you don't wish to recall. Although the subconscious and unconscious have direct links to each other and deal with similar things, the unconscious mind is really the cellar, the underground library of all your memories, habits, and behaviors. It is the storehouse of all your deep seated emotions that have been programmed since birth. The important point to remember is that we cannot, by choice, remember anything in our unconscious without some special event or technique. The subconscious, on the other hand, is almost the same, but the major difference is we can choose to remember. The memories are closer to the surface and more easily accessible with a little focus.

HOW THOUGHTS ARE FORMED AND HOW TO CHANGE THEM

The following is a short, basic description of how thought are formed. The brain consists predominantly of neurons, or 'brain cells.' A neuron is an electrically charged cell that processes and transmits information by electro-chemical signaling. Each neuron is connected to 10 000 other neurons, passing signals to each other via synaptic connections. The connections between neurons are not fixed, it can change over time. The more signals sent between two neurons, the stronger the connection grows.

Thought are generated by your conscious mind, and when you think a thought, a neuron sends a signal to another neuron through the synapses in your brain, forming a link, or a path if you like, and each time you think that same thought, the path is set deeper and stronger, like a little footpath on your way to the river, and to change that thought once it has been formed is not easy, but it is possible. How?

By replacing it with a new thought, like choosing to walk on the newly formed road right next to the footpath to the river. If you stop walking on the footpath of the thought that is not shaping the future you want, it will disappear in time. Just like the repeated unwanted thoughts became part of your subconscious and unconscious minds through habits and belief systems, so the new thought can become part of you and eventually replace the unwanted thoughts, habits and belief systems.

Dr. Joe Dispenza says in his book, 'Breaking the habit of being yourself,' 'The gift of neuroplasticity (the brain's ability to rewire and create new circuits at any age as a result of input from the environment and our conscious intentions) is that we can create a new level of mind. There's a sort of neurological 'out with the old, in with the new,' a process that neuroscientists call pruning and sprouting. It's what I call unlearning and learning, and it creates the opportunity for us to rise above our current limitations and to be greater than our conditioning or circumstances.'

CREATE YOUR NEW REALITY

Based on the above, it seems not *too* difficult to change your bad habits or thoughts and replace them with the opposite, more positive ones, but it takes hard work and a lot of dedication to persist. Life tends to get in the way of your plans if you do not consciously work at it every day. John Kehoe says that 'we are either consciously creating our lives, or we are reacting to it.' Now is the time to deliberately start creating the life you want by practicing your new future in a focused manner.

GRATITUDE - THEY KEY TO UNLOCK ABUNDANCE

Gratitude for what you already have, no matter how big or how small, is a sure way of bringing more things into your life. Gratitude is linked to the law of 'what you sow, you will reap' and the law of attraction.

Gratitude emanates a pure frequency which attracts abundance and stops the perpetual feeling that you do not have enough. When you feel you do not have enough, unfortunately you wouldn't ever have enough. That is how it works. Constantly striving to arrive at the place where you actually have enough will remain just that; striving, because although you think your 'wanting and striving' is physical, it is not. It is spiritual and emotional as well, and you are going round and round, like in a circle - getting nowhere. You need to stop and decide you are happy and that you actually have enough – be grateful! A feeling of scarcity can cause you to succumb to external influences and pressures to give up and forget who you really are. It will stop you from claiming your rightful place and owning the space you occupy. It will cause feelings of despondency which is a sure killer of joy and happiness.

'Our preoccupation with seeking inner satisfaction from external sources keeps us on a never-ending merry-go-round of pursuits and distractions, always waiting for, and expecting happiness to come to us from the outside. After the temporary pleasure or sense of accomplishment dissipates and wears off, as it most certainly will, we find ourselves once again pursuing the next fix. The miracle of practicing gratitude is that it reverses this pattern of looking outwardly for satisfaction, and instantly puts us in touch with all the many gifts and blessings already present in our life. We shift from spinning in perpetual motion on the wheel of seeking happiness from the outside-in to generating happiness from the inside-out. This practice is easy to do and can be done anywhere and any time. The main thing is just to begin to weave this practice more and more often, and more and more regularly, into your life. Both ancient teachings and modern medical research agree that one of the quickest, most direct routes to restoring harmony and balance in your life is to foster gratitude and appreciation. The moment you shift from a mindset of negativity or judgment to one of appreciation, there are immediate effects at many levels of your being: Brain function becomes more balanced, harmonized, and supple; your heart begins to pump in a much more coherent and harmonious rhythm; and biochemical changes trigger a host of healthful responses throughout your body. Especially in difficult times, remembering to return to gratitude is a radical life-affirming act that builds your capacity for resilience.' Huffingtonpost.com.

There is always something to be grateful for, whether it is big or small. All you need to do is look around you. There will always be people who has more money, a bigger house, a smarter car, or whatever material things you are able to see in the material world, but there will also always be people that has less; people with no money, no home, and no car. You need to be thankful for what you have. That is the beginning of greater things that will appear in your life.

YOU, THE UNIVERSE AND GOD

Because you are a vibrational being, you are connected to everyone else on this planet, and to the universe. Our biggest mistake is that we think our thoughts, words, emotions and actions do not have an impact on our circumstances, environment and the rest of the planet, but it does.

Where does your responsibility start? It starts with you. Take responsibility for your life, your thoughts, words, emotions and actions. People tend to blame God, or the universe, or anything but themselves for their circumstances, especially when it is bad. They will conveniently forget to blame anything outside of themselves when things are going well.

Because you are connected to the universe, you are connected to God. It is your choice, however, if you want to accept Him or not, but even if you reject God, you are still connected to Him, one way or the other. Look at the how the stars, constellations and milky-ways are constructed. Look below the sea and in the human body and mind - you will find similarities, coincidence? I think not.

HOW I PRACTICE MY NEW FUTURE EVERY DAY

I started my journey of creating a new future for myself by reading self-help and motivational books. I listened to relevant motivational talks and meditated while listening to binaural beats that boosted my serotonin, dopamine, oxytocin and endorphin levels. I believe that it's possible that some people are born with a chemical imbalance in their bodies that causes them to 'under produce happy chemicals.' I suspect that I might've been one of those people. I also started to take deliberate note of my thoughts and my body language, and I gave attention to the words I spoke.

As I progressed, I implemented the following to help me reach my goals, whether on a physical, emotional or spiritual level. I am still reminding myself of the following truths on a daily basis by putting the phrases on my phone with the alarm set at a different time for each one, and each time the alarm goes off, I read the phrase out loud or in my mind. Eventually I woke up in the mornings with one of these truths echoing in my mind, which proofed to me that it is possible to change your thoughts about yourself and everything else. It is possible to claim your rightful place and own the space you occupy by practicing your new future every day. Here are my phrases: (you can use your own phrases where you have different goals)

- 08:00: I am a full-time author and artist. I a calm and collected. I am worthy of happiness and I do not have to justify my existence. I am exactly where I am supposed to be.
- 08:30: I remember to love myself and others. I accept myself unconditionally and I intend to feel good. I am already in my mind where I intended to be.
- 09:00: I claim my rightful place, step into the right-now-zone and I practice my new future every day. I give myself permission to be successful in everything I do. Money flows to me easily.
- 09:30: I believe in myself, I have nothing to loose. I am neither below, nor above anyone. I am kind and compassionate but I do not interfere with God's work.
- 10:00: By placing new 'I am's' in my imagination, my future dreams become my present reality. I am persistent and patient, knowing all will arrive at the perfect time.
- 10:30: I am love, I am loving kindness and I am forgiving, I am enough. I feel prosperous. I eat healthy and I practice the feeling of living a happy life.
- 11:00: I stand up for myself. I am one with God, I am worthy, I am infinite and validate myself, and I do not have to wait for permission from anyone. I am free.

By 11:00 in the morning, on a daily basis, I reminded myself of the things that I regard as important in my life. Repetition is the key. That is how new neural pathways get formed. These pathways sets into habits and habits rule your life. You can make use of a notebook to write down the things you have to remind yourself about and read it to yourself every day. You can read it when you want and as many times as you feel is important, and you do not have to read your phrases all at once, spread them out. You can also read it out loud, or in your mind. The spoken word carries vibration, but when you read it in your mind, energy is released, so either way you win, as long as you keep on practicing your new future EVERY DAY!

THE STEP INTO THE RIGHT-NOW-ZONE METHOD

I have created the 'Step into the Right-now-zone Method' to assist me in becoming aware of my thought-patterns, my breathing, my posture and my feelings. Why is it important to become aware? Because our constant thought-patterns solidify into habits and beliefs and they are difficult to change once they are set into your subconscious mind. Your breathing and posture has an effect on how you feel and your feelings determine your outlook on life, which again has as effect on your thought-patterns. Can you see how important it is to become self-aware? The Step into the Right-now-zone Method works as follows:

Whenever I feel irritated, agitated, frustrated, depressed, lonely, angry, or any other negative feeling, I close my eyes and imagine that I am wearing a robe that is soaked in negative emotions, I can feel the weight of it. I then take a deep breath and visualize myself giving one big step forward (you can if you wish literally take one step forward) while I leave whatever is bothering me behind by dropping the robe on the floor behind me. It slips off from my back – I discard the robe and I step away from it while it disappears. At that moment I do not even try to analyze what exactly it was that bothered me because every moment that pass is in the past and should not have an effect on my life anymore. That means that everything gets left behind; including guilt over something that I might've said or did wrong.

You have to learn to forgive yourself. By stepping into the now, you free yourself from whatever burden is holding you back. You free yourself from the past, even if it is as much as one minute ago. The Step into the Right-now-zone Method forces you to bring your attention to what is at hand, the now. Whatever you were thinking, doing or feeling before you took the step ceases to exist and you will be able to bring your focus back to what is important.

Due to becoming self-aware and more relaxed, your mind is then able to figure out what it was that made you feel negative or stressed, and when you know what it was, you will be able to rectify it if rectifying is required. If you, for instance, felt depressed because of a constant thought like, 'I don't think I can do it,' you will be able to deliberately rectify it with a thought like, 'I can do it. I believe in myself.'

What I do after I stepped into the 'now,' is deliberately implanting positive thoughts or phrases into my mind using self-talk, either silently in my thoughts or out loud. I use phrases like, 'I am so blessed, I love myself, I am very proud of all my accomplishments, I am always in the right place at the right time, nature is wonderfully beautiful (then I deliberately look because I love nature!),' or I'll say one of the 'I am' powerful phrases, 'I am worthy, I am love, I am abundant,' or any other 'I am' phrase, or 'The whole universe supports me.' There are so many phrases to choose from.

Continue to practice this method until it feels natural. Everything in life can be learned through repetition. I would love to receive your feedback on the Step into the Right-now-zone Method. Please address your comments to: claimrightfulplace@gmail.com.

THE KEY FACTORS

- By vibrating at a certain frequency, you unconsciously attract circumstances to match your current frequency. If you want to attract different circumstances, you will have to change your frequency.
- Accept yourself and other people unconditionally.
- Instead of judging yourself and others, choose to become an observer of behaviors.
- Constantly forgive yourself and others.
- Believe in yourself. If you don't believe in yourself, you will be unable to trust your instincts, your inner being, and you will merely drift through life, and you'll be tossed around by the currents of existence and circumstances.
- Expect good results - expect to receive good things in life and to succeed in everything you do.
- Don't give your power away! Decide to persist, even if you feel scared.
- Awareness is the key to change. You cannot make changes if you are unaware that something is wrong or amiss.
- You must be relaxed to be able to receive, therefore, detach yourself emotionally from the outcome.

- Accept that, in the physical reality of life, good and bad is part of one whole.
- If you find it difficult to deal with disappointments, you set yourself up for failure.
- The laws of attraction are linked to the law of sow and reap. If there is no seed in the soil of your garden, which is your mind, there will be no harvest.
  - You get to choose the seeds you sow.
  - Good, positive thoughts equal a good harvest.
  - Bad, negative thoughts equal a bad harvest.
  - Self-discipline is the key to success.
- Fear is a natural part of being human.
  - It can have a negative effect on your physical, emotional, and spiritual wellbeing.
  - Fear does not have to dominate your life in a negative way.
  - When you experience fear, breathe in deeply and remind yourself that you are busy practicing for your new future so you can claim your rightful place and own the space you occupy.
- Despondency can be dangerous.
- Not all thoughts that enter your mind are the truth. You are able to disregard a thought and replace it with one that suits you.
- Change is not easy, and it is impossible to change years of bad thinking, negative words, and harmful emotions in a few weeks' time. Change takes time and patience. Be patient with yourself!
- Gratitude is a key that unlocks abundance in your life.

- The world (man-created, worldly systems) wants you to be suppressed and depressed. It is time to wake up!

- You will experience resistance within yourself when you try to change your negative thoughts, words and emotions, but you must persist!

- Become aware that there is more to life than meets the eye.

- Your ego wants to believe and declare its independent isolation, but it is a false notion. You are not alone. People have an effect on each other, whether you believe it or not.

- Ask yourself; am I spiritually awake? If not, what must I do to attain spiritual wakefulness?

- You are worthy to claim your rightful place on this earth and to own the space you occupy!

ABOUT THE AUTHOR

 Madeleen Theron (pen name; Madeleen Viljoen-Theron) was born in 1965 in Pretoria, South Africa, and was raised in a little town with a mountain backdrop called, Mountain View. Her passion for reading started at a very young age and caused her to get into trouble when her mom found her hiding storybooks inside of her study books. To her the library was like a second home and the stories she read transported her to another world, one where she felt more at home than in the real world.

She had a clear preference for fiction and fantasy and it is therefore not unexpected that her first published books were for children. *Sparky the Dragon-horse* was written as a six-book series. Both of the first two titles; *Fired Up* and *Daddy's Boy* were published as 32-pages, fully illustrated, full-color books by Fantasi Books, 2011. The series was originally written in Afrikaans and translated into English.

Some of her poems, written both in Afrikaans and English, have been published in various anthologies of verse. Madeleen is also a proud contributor to *Rympies vir pikkies en peuters* (*Rhymes for toddlers*), Tafelberg Publishers, 2015. Although always an ardent reader and writer,

Madeleen started to take the possibility of becoming a published writer only serious at an advanced age after her son, Vincente, was a bit older. The stories inside her were looking for a way to make themselves known to the world.

She was fortunate to have the opportunity to write children's stories for Maskew Miller Longman and Oxford University Press, and has short stories published, titled; *Boggomsbaai se diewevangers (Boggomsbaai's thieve catchers)*, with Nasau Via Africa, 2013 and *I Can Forgive* – Breaking the Silence – Love & Revolution - POWA Women's Writing Project, 2010. She also does freelance evaluations and editing work for publishing companies and did a book translation from English to Afrikaans, titled; *Created to be his Help Meet* (Debbie Pearl), 2014. Madeleen is also a passionate watercolor painter and would in future love to go over to painting in other mediums as well.

She realized she had a passion to help people overcome the obstacles that hold them back from living a full and happy life and since she was struggling with her own self confidence and sense of self-worth and self-love, she became an dedicated seeker of true liberation and was first lead to the works of Dr. Wayne W Dyer, John Kehoe, other authors of Hay House, and the work of Dawn Clark. After more than ten years of fighting the good fight of truly finding herself, she was able to produce a book that is very close to her heart, because it is the culmination of everything that she's been struggling with. She has partnered up with Balboa Press (Hay House) to self-publish her book, *Claim your Rightful place* in 2017.

It is Madeleen's dream to create wider platforms where people can learn how to believe in themselves and in the power of God, and where they can learn how to teach their own children from a young age to do the same. She wants to focus these teachings on people that are economically disadvantaged.

Madeleen currently resides in the Western Cape, South Africa.

Printed in the United States
By Bookmasters